"This book belongs on every coffee table in the state of Ohio."—Kristina Estle, Museum Director, Underground Railroad Museum Ohio Valley. (Flushing, Ohio.)

"How wonderful to have a book shed light on our local hero, John B. Mahan, and on the volatile era in which he lived. The amount of detail was amazing. It is great having such a reference."—Sandra Purdy, Sardinia (Ohio) Historical Society.

"Readers will feel like they have been transported back to the 1830-40s. By book's end, you will feel like you personally know Mahan. He was a humble Christian who lived his faith with courage and conviction."—Thomas Homans, Principal, Christian Community Center Homeschool Co-op, inner-city Baltimore, Maryland.

"Despite all his tribulations, this Methodist preacher remained true to the religious faith that led him to work unceasingly against the "Slave Power." This story of righteous perseverance deserves to be told, and Daniel J. Vance tells it very well."—Dr. William Vance Trollinger, Jr., Professor of History, University of Dayton.

In honor of Joe and Marye Vance
Sardinia High Class of 1948

Other Daniel J. Vance Books
Available at LULU.COM

Unique Mankato Stories

The War!

Lake Moobegon Days

Rev. John B. Mahan: Ohio Abolitionist, National Martyr

Rev. John B. Mahan

Ohio Abolitionist
National Martyr

Daniel J. Vance

Advance Creative
Box 154
Vernon Center, MN, 56090

Rev. John B. Mahan: Ohio Abolitionist, National Martyr

Copyright © 2025 by Daniel J. Vance

First printing 2025

For information about bulk or bookstore purchases, contact danieljvance@gmail.com

Printed in the United States of America

ISBN: 978-0-9672014-2-9

CONTENTS

AUTHOR'S INTRODUCTION   8

Part One
THE OVERALL MOOD   18
SARDINIA & SOUTHWEST OHIO   33
THE PEOPLE   54
THE NEWSPAPERS   67

Part Two
IMPRISONMENT   72
THE FIRST TRIAL   90
A NATION REACTS   133

Part Three
THE SECOND TRIAL   153
THE THIRD TRIAL   166
THE FINAL YEARS   177
THE FOURTH TRIAL   186

Part Four
MAHAN'S EULOGY   194
WHAT WE DON'T KNOW   201

NOTES   205
BIBLIOGRAPHY   220
NAME INDEX   224
ABOUT THE AUTHOR   228
ACKNOWLEDGEMENTS   229

Setting the Stage
AUTHOR'S INTRODUCTION

Sardinia, Ohio, doesn't cover much ink on a road map, just a round black blip forty miles east of Cincinnati, in what until the last couple decades was prime burley tobacco country. White Oak Creek meanders through and around Sardinia village limits, and downstream passes just outside Georgetown, the boyhood home of Ulysses S. Grant, before emptying at Higginsport on the Ohio River. It's surprisingly beautiful country that includes a covered bridge near Sardinia and serpentine roads that have no end.

The village of Sardinia has more than one thousand friendly residents, and in terms of businesses has a Tractor Supply outlet, Manning Packing (locally raised, grain-fed, and antibiotic-free angus beef), two gas stations, a laundromat, and a perky coffee shop.

While motoring old two-lane Ohio State Route 32 from Cincinnati into Sardinia, Ohio, as a boy, and later, an adult, I would read every time passing the village historical marker that Sardinia had been an "Underground Railroad Station" and home to "Rev. John B. Mahan," a "Noted Abolitionist."

I was curious.

Many of my ancestors settled Sardinia in the early 1800s, all my grandparents and great grandparents hailed from the Sardinia area, both my parents graduated from Sardinia High School, and I personally knew many Sardinians; and yet in all my years of regularly visiting I never once heard a word spoken about Rev. John B. Mahan. *The* Rev. John B. Mahan.

It was as if this man had never existed.

I sometimes heard Grandma Mignerey, Grandma Vance

or Uncle Stan spin stories of an underground "slave tunnel" reaching from "downtown" Sardinia to a bank on White Oak Creek to help fugitive blacks escape slavery. But nothing else. The dearth of information surprised me given Grandma Vance, especially, had an incredible memory and often shared what she knew about Sardinia, her life-long home. However, not once did she say her family had owned a building in which Rev. John B. Mahan had actually lived. Not once did Grandma Mignerey mention her home at 121 North Main literally was a stone's throw from homes owned years earlier by Dr. Isaac Beck and Josiah Moore (125 and 126 North Main), both Sardinia abolitionists and Mahan associates.

Regarding my childhood experience of regularly visiting Sardinia and not hearing any native Sardinian ever mention Mahan, I could use an oft-quoted Bible passage: "A prophet is not without honor except in his hometown."

Rev. John Bennington Mahan was a great American abolitionist and recognized as such in his day by abolitionist leaders: by their words, the trusted positions they gave him within the emerging movement, the effect his actions had on state and federal politics, and in the way they honored him and his family following his death.

For example, James G. Birney, co-founder of the Ohio Anti-Slavery Society, 1840 and 1844 Liberty Party U.S. Presidential candidate, former Kentucky and Alabama State House member, and founding editor of the anti-slavery newspaper *The Philanthropist*, said this of Mahan in *James G. Birney and His Times*:

> John B. Mahan, a tall, muscular, raw-boned, stalwart, and

swarthy man of middle age, had long been one of the most active friends of fugitive negroes. He was a farmer and local Methodist preacher. He had not been in a slave state since childhood; but, from about 1820, any man fleeing from bondage could rely upon his hospitality and protection. His strength and courage, tested in sundry conflicts with slave-catchers, had given them a salutary respect for him.... In 1826 a close connection was formed by him and his associates with Levi Coffin and other Quakers in Wayne County, Indiana. He knew reliable friends in the counties adjoining his own to whom he could confide fugitives.... Mahan was a taciturn man; he was no boaster, but his somber piety and bravery would have endeared him to Oliver Cromwell. Before the [1835 Ohio Anti-Slavery Society] convention was over, he was appreciated by his fellow-members.

The year 1820, noted above as when Mahan began helping fugitive blacks through Sardinia, predated Rev. John Rankin becoming pastor in Ripley by two years.

The works of Rev. Rankin have received worldwide acclaim, and rightfully so, primarily for his having been one of America's greatest abolitionists—not to mention being an exceptional Presbyterian pastor over a forty-year period. He wrote *Letters on Slavery*, which was published in book form in 1826 and in abolitionist William Lloyd Garrison's anti-slavery newspaper *The Liberator* in 1832. Rankin later addressed and challenged attendees in Cincinnati, including Harriet Beecher Stowe, at the famous 1834 Lane Seminary Debates. He co-founded the Ohio Anti-Slavery Society in 1835. His Underground Railroad line helped perhaps thousands of fugitive blacks find freedom.

Harriet Beecher Stowe's association with Rankin provided background material for *Uncle Tom's Cabin*, the wildly popular 1852 book that cemented Northern opposition to slavery. To Harriet Beecher Stowe, President Abraham Lincoln supposedly said, "So you're the little woman who wrote the book that made this great war!" Also, the Rankin House overlooking the Ohio River in Ripley today is a National Historic Landmark. We could continue on.

That said, Mahan also played a major role as a co-founder of the Ohio Anti-Slavery Society.

Nationally, due to his legal trials, he became known as an abolitionist who made enormous personal sacrifices for the *cause*. While unjustly imprisoned in Kentucky for his first legal trial, especially, his personal letters and the trial proceedings were published in newspapers all over the nation. In all, he was pulled through the mud of four unfair trials, perhaps the first-ever American to become a victim of "lawfare," i.e., being embarrassed, emotionally harassed, and bankrupted through legal means by an opponent.

In the early years, starting about 1834, Sardinia was the first "whistle" stop on Rankin's Underground Railroad line, about twenty miles north of Ripley. From here, Mahan and dozens of Sardinia co-workers, including Dr. Isaac Beck, John Hudson, Josiah Moore, and the Pettijohn family, helped guide fugitive blacks north, mostly to Canada.

Mahan, like Rankin, lectured against slavery and helped organize local anti-slavery societies. They both became lightning rods for anti-abolitionist sentiment. They inspired thousands, but many more thousands passionately hated them, e.g., both had pricey bounties placed on their heads.

At least one Kentucky slave owner was on a personal vendetta to make Mahan into an example. Mahan assuredly paid the price: he suffered financially, his wife and young family grieved, and he languished bound in heavy iron shackles in a Kentucky prison for more than two chilly months while awaiting his first trial. It took a toll on his health.

Most of the legal cases involving Mahan, from 1838-1843, garnered significant attention in Northern and Southern newspapers. His plight certainly raised awareness for immediate (rather than *gradual*) abolition, in an age when immediate abolitionists were a small minority of the general population.

To name a few newspapers covering Mahan's plight, mostly over his first three trials: *The Democrat* (Huntsville, Alabama), *Bangor Daily Whig and Courier* (Maine), *Tri-Weekly Nashville Union, Alexandria Gazette* (Virginia), *Vermont Telegraph, Daily Herald and Gazette* (Cleveland), *Pittsburgh Post-Gazette, Georgia Journal and Messenger* (Macon), *Kentucky Gazette* (Lexington), *Democratic Free Press* (Detroit), *The Evening Post* (New York City), *Richmond Enquirer* (Virginia), *The Philanthropist* (Cincinnati), and of course, *The Liberator* (Boston). There were very many more.

Many people of that era believed public reaction to Mahan's imprisonment prior to his first trial decided the outcome of the 1838 Ohio gubernatorial election involving Whig incumbent Gov. Joseph Vance. It was Vance who played a major role in the chain of events leading to Mahan's Ohio arrest and wrongful Kentucky imprisonment—a chain that started only two months before the election. Vance lost by just 5,000-plus votes statewide.

Within weeks after Mahan's first trial ended, the U.S.

Senate and U.S. House in December 1838 began passing a number of anti-abolitionist and pro-slavery resolutions to stop dissent and build a support base for preserving the "peculiar" institution. (Mahan's case was but one issue of many leading up to this backlash happening; but for many pro-slavery people Mahan was the last straw.)

For example, one passed 1838 U.S. House resolution actually snuffed out *any and all* future House debate on the slavery issue—for a while, at least. That resolution passed 126 to 78. A House member afterwards couldn't even mention slavery on the House floor, in a country with supposed free speech rights.

> ....and that every petition, memorial, resolution, proposition, or paper, touching or relating in any way, or to any extent whatever, to Slavery, as aforesaid, or the abolition thereof, shall, on the presentation thereof, without any further action thereon, be laid upon the table, without being debated, printed or referred."

After the Whigs and Vance lost the 1838 Ohio election, Ohio Democrats seized power top to bottom, from the state legislature to the governor's office. In the months following the first Mahan trial—while encouraged and empowered by aggressive Kentucky lobbyists—Ohio lawmakers enacted the controversial 1839 Ohio Fugitive Slave Law aimed at trying to prohibit what John B. Mahan had just done.

The Ohio House also in early 1839 passed a resolution that no doubt pointed fingers at Mahan, stating, "That the schemes of the Abolitionists, for the pretended happiness of the slaves, are, in the opinion of this General Assembly, wild, delusive, and fanatical; and have a direct tendency to destroy the harmony of the Union, to rivet the chain of the slaves, and to destroy the perpetuity of our free institutions."

The Slave Power tried making an example out of Mahan to dissuade others from joining the abolitionist cause. That much will become quite clear from reading this book. In this they would only partially succeed. They did symbolically tar-and-feather Mahan, and damage his health, family life, and pocket-book; however, they also inadvertently transformed him into a national martyr for abolitionism, thus advancing the cause.

Now, to the other side of Mahan. Besides being an important abolitionist, Rev. John B. Mahan was *Reverend* John B. Mahan, a Methodist "local preacher." His Christian faith was the engine on his section of the Underground Railroad. He kept his Christian faith firm in the face of relentless persecution, as shown in his determination to continue fighting and not giving in, in his letters from prison published nationally, and his ever-present fervor until his premature death at age forty-three. This *determination* in the face of adversity can be an excellent example to any modern American of any background facing any difficulty.

From that horrible Washington (now Maysville), Kentucky, prison cell in 1838, while bound in shackles, he wrote his wife, eight children, and friends in loving, encouraging, positive tones, trying to uplift their spirits—thinking first of them rather than himself—the same way he wrote his last will and testament a few years later during his third trial. He also spoke truth to authority while in prison, including to Ohio Governor Vance.

Today, Sardinia Cemetery rests along Sardinia-

Mowrystown Road, on this quiet village's northeastern edge. White Oak Creek is two hundred yards away. At least to this author, the cemetery's historic iron fence is a visual reminder and testimony to Mahan's iron-willed desire for equal rights for every American. In the more mature section of the cemetery, among spreading shade trees, surrounded by gravesites of abolitionist co-workers, the gravestone that marks Mahan's 1844 burial reads, "A Victim to the Slave Power." This author has witnessed those true words with his own eyes. Permit me to show you the brave heart of this man.

Daniel J. Vance (2025)

ABOVE: Sardinia historical marker gracing Old State Route 32, on the southwest entry into the village. *BELOW*: Mahan's "Temperance Tavern," built mid-1830s, used in 2025 as "The Underground Café," at Winchester and Main. (Photos: Randi York)

ABOVE: Sardinia Cemetery. John B. Mahan grave. "A Victim to the Slave Power." (Photo: Randi York.) BELOW: John Bennington Mahan.

Setting the Stage: The Overall Mood
CHAPTER ONE

Prior to the national excitement over Rev. John B. Mahan's first trial in late 1838—the first of four that would make him an abolitionist martyr—the collective citizenries of Southwest Ohio and Northern Kentucky already were at boiling point due to pro- and anti-abolitionist agitation. Mahan was in the midst. He *experienced* and *felt* it. You could even say he, and abolitionists like him, were the reason for it.

On the pro-abolitionist side in Southwest Ohio, primarily, was an armada of Christian preachers, mostly all Presbyterian and zealous, though some Quaker, Mahan a Methodist, and others, with most of the Presbyterians having emigrated to Ohio in recent decades due to opposing slavery. These preachers, mainly of Southern origins, *knew* the soul of the institution, in part because they had witnessed the effects first-hand. They had seen slavery shackles with their eyes, and heard groans with their ears. By the mid-1830s, these preachers, mainly, were developing the logistics of what would become their section of the Underground Railroad. Theirs was a network of like-minded co-workers.

Secondarily on the pro-abolitionist side were Ohio settlers who had emigrated from Kentucky and other slavery states solely due to Ohio being "free." These Ohioans were a minority, and not all by any means were abolitionists. Some supported the American Colonization Society, for example, which wanted to resettle free blacks to Africa. In addition, Kentucky had pro-abolitionists too, who kept quiet or operated behind-the-scenes.

The anti-abolitionist side, primarily, had an army of

undeniably angry, and often wealthy, Kentucky slave holders, and their fervent supporters. They were directly across the two- to three-hundred-yard-wide Ohio River, waving their fists, and furious at Ohio preachers and their congregants who were helping their property north towards freedom.

Also, not a small number of Ohio whites feared blacks could take away their jobs in the event abolition actually occurred. Other Ohioans tried catching and returning fugitives for the reward. All this held true in Cincinnati, the nation's sixth largest city in the 1830s, only forty miles west of Sardinia. The "Queen City," at that time, essentially was a Southern city anchored on free soil. Many Cincinnati whites had emigrated from the slave states Virginia and Kentucky, and had carried those sympathies with them.

In many respects, at least in the 1830s, as for the issue of slavery, the battle waging in Ohio and Kentucky was one of David versus Goliath, with the abolitionists being "David."

Given the Goliath (a Kentucky slave owner named Greathouse) Mahan would have to battle from 1838-43, you could call John B. Mahan a "David," too.

Of the two groups, federal law in the 1830s firmly was on the slave owners' side, a fact which complicated the issue for some abolitionists. For example, it was difficult for some abolitionist pastors to take a moral stand against slavery and help fugitive blacks while using the Bible as the basis of their argument, when the Bible itself taught Christians to honor earthly authorities. Slave owners often called abolitionists lawbreakers, which, technically, they sometimes were.

Being an abolitionist in the 1830s was risky business, in large measure because of the federal Fugitive Slave Act of

1793, which allowed for the agent of a slave holder to seize or arrest a fugitive slave *anywhere* in the United States or its territories. Upon arrest, the agent could take the slave before any Circuit or District Court judge or any magistrate of any county, city or incorporated town. Upon oral testimony or an affidavit from the agent saying the slave "had fled, owed service or labor," the judge or magistrate had a *duty* to help the agent return the fugitive to his master. The slave could not testify on his or her own behalf. The Act also declared that anyone "knowingly and willingly" obstructing and hindering the agent, or rescuing, harboring or concealing a known fugitive, could be fined $500. President George Washington signed the law.

Some abolitionists obeyed the letter of the law by never asking fugitives if in fact they were fugitives. If challenged in court over whether they had concealed a *known* fugitive, for example, they could simply say they had given meals and directions to a weary, needy traveler—applying the Golden Rule.

That legal landscape affected the Ohio Constitutional Convention in Chillicothe in 1802, the meeting that would decide whether slavery would be legal when Ohio became a state in 1803. Ephraim Cutler, one of thirty-five convention delegates, opposed slavery. The Northwest Ordinance of 1787 had forbidden slavery, he said, and Ohio's constitution should too. They vigorously debated. Cutler's proposal to outlaw slavery passed the state constitutional convention by one vote—his own, made while being sick and having to be carried in.

Though Ohio's constitution officially forbid slavery, the state legislature in 1804 and 1807 would enact very strict laws to prevent the state's *free* blacks from having anything close to the same rights as whites. These laws created an Ohio social landscape in which free blacks or "mulattos" could not vote, attend public school, hold political office, serve on a jury, testify against a white person in court, or be in a militia.

The 1807 Act, Section 1, labeled "An act regulating black and mulatto persons," may have been the most restrictive part of all these laws. It virtually assured that most fugitive slaves passing through Ohio (or Sardinia, for that matter) would seriously consider moving on to Canada rather than stay. For the modern reader, and regarding Section 1 (below), imagine being unable to move into Ohio unless first posting bond, needing a local clerk to approve where you could live, having to be of "good" behavior as determined by the same clerk in order to stay, and if "non-compliant" being removed *immediately* from your place of residence.

> Be it enacted by the general assembly of the state of Ohio, that no negro or mulatto person shall be permitted to emigrate into and settle within this state, unless such negro or mulatto person shall, within twenty days thereafter, enter into bond with two or more freehold sureties, in the penal sum of five hundred dollars, before the clerk of the court of common pleas of the county in which such negro or mulatto may wish to reside (to be approved of by the clerk) conditioned for the good behavior of such negro or mulatto, and moreover to pay for the support of such person, in case he, she or they should thereafter be found within any township in this state, unable to support themselves. And if any negro or mulatto person shall migrate into this state, and not comply with the provisions of this act, it shall be the duty

of the overseers of the poor of the township where such negro or mulatto person may be found to remove immediately, such black or mulatto person, in the same manner, as is required in the case of paupers.

Harsh Kentucky laws regarding enslaved blacks made Ohio laws towards free blacks seem milquetoast. By the mid-1830s, in Kentucky, for example, enslaved blacks could not leave home without carrying a master's permission note, could not carry a weapon, could not trade at market without master consent, were classified as "real estate" in settling estates, and could not even work on a steamboat. Freed slaves at all times had to carry a certificate of freedom. Boats could not transport slaves across the Ohio River without master consent, with boat owners fined $200 for non-compliance. In 1834, a new Kentucky law even made giving or selling liquor to a slave illegal.

The Kentucky Slave Stealing Statute of 1830 fired up this tense atmosphere on both sides of the Ohio River among Kentucky slave owners and Ohio abolitionists, and would eventually be the *sine qua non* of Rev. Mahan's 1838 arrest. The Statute took the federal Fugitive Slave Law of 1793 to a whole new level of enforcement. It was disturbing to abolitionists, to say the least. The statute read, in full:

> That if any person not having lawful, or color of claim thereto, shall be guilty of seducing or enticing any slave to leave his lawful owner or possessor; and to escape to parts without the limits of the state, to any of the other states, or a foreign county; or shall make, or finish, or aid and assist in making or furnishing a forged pass of freedom, or any other forged paper purporting to be a deed of emancipation, or will, or other instrument,

liberating, or purporting to liberate, any slave, or shall in any manner aid or assist such slave in making his escape from such owner or possessor, to another state, or foreign country; every person so offending, shall, on conviction, be sentenced to confinement in the jail and penitentiary of this commonwealth, a period not less than two years, nor more than twenty years.

Enslaved Kentucky blacks were far more apt than enslaved Deep South blacks to flee their masters for a number of reasons, not the least of which was the proximity of free state Ohio across the river. In low or frozen water, a fugitive enslaved black literally could walk across the Ohio River to freedom. By 1830, also, Kentucky slave owners were becoming slave exporters to other states, especially of teens and younger men to the Deep South. For example, the black population of Kentucky from 1830-60 fell from 25 to 21 percent, mostly due to these sales. The possibility of being sold "...left borderland slaves with two options: take a chance at freedom by heading north or endure a lifetime of servitude and die a slave in the Deep South."

The fear of being sold "Down South" and away from family and friends eventually became a major reason many slaves fled north. It was a loss of income for slave masters. Another issue motivating Kentucky enslaved persons to flee was their limited life span, which was an observable fact to them. For example, in Mason County, home of Maysville, out of 2,119 male slaves noted in the 1840 U.S. Census, only 281 were over age thirty-six. The motive for some slaves fleeing maybe had less to do with life quality and more with simply staying alive.

It was in this volatile environment for abolitionists in the

1830s, and within a year after the Ohio Anti-Slavery Society formed in 1835, that James G. Birney—the same Birney who publicly recognized Mahan for his abolitionist work—began publishing an abolitionist newspaper for the Ohio Anti-Slavery Society, *The Philanthropist*. It initiated printing in New Richmond, Ohio, on February 12, 1836, downriver from Rev. John Rankin and Ripley. Soon, however, Birney moved the Society newspaper into tempestuous, Southern-minded Cincinnati, and that is when all hell broke loose.

Birney should have realized in advance the staunch opposition he would face, and the consequences he and the organization would pay. As an abolitionist who had lived most his life in the South, i.e., Kentucky and Alabama, he had known the milieu and should have been able to gauge the reaction.

Events in that year already had troubled many abolitionists. Only a couple months before the 1836 Cincinnati Riots, the U.S. formally admitted Arkansas, a slave state, into the Union; and the Republic of Texas was forming as a new *country* that would allow slavery. Some abolitionists feared Texas would become a pro-slavery U.S. state. Some abolitionists felt as if they were losing.

The entire sequence of events regarding the 1836 Cincinnati Riots used here was republished in the *Carroll Free Press (Ohio)*, from a prior *Cincinnati Whig* article. (Editors republishing other editor's articles in the 1830s was a common practice.) Dozens, if not hundreds, of similar incidents of violence could be brought forth here to illustrate the 1830s societal push and shove over abolition, and the toxic Southwest Ohio environment for abolitionists in the years preceding Mahan's 1838 trial—*in order to set the stage for you.*

However, to this author, no single incident painted a picture of such open hatred in Southwest Ohio towards abolitionists, with such vitriol, and on such a grand scale, as the 1836 Cincinnati Riots. It was within a similar type of hornet's nest of anti-abolitionist sentiment Rev. John B. Mahan was shepherding fugitive blacks through Sardinia to Canada. Mahan himself had many enemies in Sardinia and Brown County, and he had to keep a sharp eye out for them. For example, the author of *The History of Brown County* opined: "The doctrines of the Abolitionists were very unpopular in this county, and those who maintained them were subjected to much odium and abuse."

The Cincinnati riots sent shock waves through the Ohio abolitionist community, including the one in Brown County, and its leaders in Cincinnati literally had to flee for their lives.

Rioters had no problem finding *The Philanthropist*. The Ohio Anti-Slavery Society had erected a massive eighteen-foot-wide banner declaring the Society's name at the corner of Main and Seventh in downtown Cincinnati.

The maelstrom started on a typically steamy Cincinnati summer night, on Thursday July 12, 1836, when a stealthy group of more than thirty anti-abolitionist mischief makers, using a ladder, scaled a wall and climbed to the headquarters roof. They forced themselves through a roof window to a room below, where they intimidated a sleeping boy. They placed clothing over him so he could not identify them. The vandals ripped copies of the next paper, destroyed ink, dismantled the printing press, stole parts. The paper had been publishing only two months in Cincinnati.

The next morning, an alarmed James G. Birney nervously

asked the Cincinnati mayor to offer a reward for the capture of the vandals. The mayor declined until a substantial deposit was made should a reward be given, and, after that having been made, the mayor issued a reward proclamation on July 18.

This grabbed the attention of agitators. A couple days later, anti-abolitionists inserted in Cincinnati's newspapers (except *The Philanthropist*) an ad declaring a public meeting to take place Saturday July 23. A thousand Cincinnatians shook their fists there with the stated goal of literally putting an end to *The Philanthropist*.

Again, Kentucky, which had legal slavery, sat only a few hundred yards away on the other side of the murky Ohio River. Technically though, since Kentucky had Ohio River ownership rights, declared in 1792, the two states literally touched where Ohio River water lapped onto the banks of the Ohio side.

The anti-abolitionist group included many respected Cincinnatians, including Morgan Neville, who had a resume a mile long that included having been part-owner of the *Pittsburgh Gazette*, Allegheny County (Penn.) sheriff, and author of "The Last of the Boatmen," a book featuring the legend of Mike Fink. (He also infamously had been involved in Aaron Burr's treasonous plot years prior.)

Noted the *Carroll Free Press*: "At that meeting resolutions were adopted condemning the spirit with which the "Philanthropist" was conducted—and [abolitionism] was denounced as unjust to the other states, as at variance with the opinions of the great mass of the population, and in direct violation of the solemn pledges given by its conductor. The meeting also resolved to use all lawful means to suppress every publication of a similar character in the city, and appointed a highly respectable committee to wait upon Birney and his associates to remonstrate with them upon the dangerous tendency of the course they were pursing, to communicate to them the actual tone of public feeling in the city, to request them by every motive of patriotism and philanthropy to desist from the publication of their paper, and to warn them that if they persist the [members of the] meeting cannot hold themselves responsible for the consequences."

This committee of Cincinnatians, mentioned above, delivered a terse message to Birney, demanding a meeting. He referred their message to the Ohio Anti-Slavery Society executive committee, whose members were all in Cincinnati and of which he was part, and the two groups passed notes back and forth before everyone gathered. The Cincinnatians refused to bend. Neither would Birney nor the Ohio Anti-Slavery Society. Anti-abolitionist Cincinnatians demanded a written reply on whether *The Philanthropist* would cease publication.

Publishing this on Monday July 30, Birney and the Society forcefully answered the anti-abolitionist mob while facing a withering challenge to their First Amendment rights.

> SIR: Whilst we feel ourselves constrained, (we) altogether decline complying with your request, as submitted last evening, to discontinue the Philanthropist. We think it but just to ourselves, and respectful to our fellow citizens generally, to offer a brief exposition of the reasons that persuade us to this course.
>
> 1—We decline complying, not so much from the fear that the particular cause in which our press is employed may be injured, but because compliance involves a tame surrender of the FREEDOM OF THE PRESS—THE

RIGHT TO DISCUSS.

2—The Philanthropist is the acknowledged organ of some twelve thousands or more of our fellow citizens of Ohio, who believe that slavery, as it exists in our country, is altogether incompatible with the permanency of her institutions; who believe that the slavery of the south or the liberty of the north must cease to exist; and who intend to do what in them lies to bring about a happy and peaceful termination of the former, and this as speedily as facts and arguments and appeals to the consciences and understandings of slaveholders can be made instrumental to effect it.

3—The Philanthropist is the only journal in this city or neighborhood through which these facts and arguments and appeals can be lawfully addressed to the community. It has been conducted with fairness and moderation, as may be abundantly proved by the acknowledgments of those who are opposed to this project. It has invited the slaveholders themselves to the use of its columns for the defence of slavery, and has given up to a republication of their arguments a large share of its space. To discontinue such a pact under existing circumstances, would be a tacit submission to the exorbitant demand of the south that *slavery* shall never more be mentioned among us.

4—We decline complying with your request, because, if it has originated among our own citizens, it is an officious and unasked for incursion on the business of others, if among the citizens of others states, it is an attempt at dictation as insolent and high-handed on their part, as a tame submission to it would be base and unmanly on ours.

5—We decline complying with your request—because we would not preclude ourselves and others from discussing in the most advantageous manner a subject which, by the acknowledgement of all, is of momentous consequence, and which is now occupying the mind of the whole nation.

6—We decline complying—because the demand is virtually the demand of slaveholders, who, having broken down all the safeguards of liberty in their own states, in order that slavery may be perpetuated, are now, for the fuller attainment of the same object, making the demand of us to follow their example.

With these reasons—to which many more might be added, did time permit—we leave the case with you; expressing, however, our firm conviction, should any disturbance of the peace occur, that you, gentlemen, must be deeply, if not almost entirely responsible for it, before the bar of social and enlightened public opinion. (The entire executive committee approved the note.)

That night, Cincinnatians witnessed enflamed violence and an utter disrespect for First Amendment rights few, if any, Americans have experienced since. About nine p.m., a lubricated mob of up to five thousand assembled around *The Philanthropist* at Main and Seventh, circling as dogs eyeing smaller prey. (Some may have been there just for the spectacle or for the fun.) Vandals, out in full view of everyone and exhibiting absolutely no fear—because they believed no Cincinnatian would intervene, and sure of their cause—kicked open office doors and tossed out printing type and materials as they would confetti. The rowdy crowd hooted them on. They shattered windows, smashed to smithereens office items, and dragged southward the main body of the printing press over manured streets and heaved the metal into the murky Ohio River at the public landing. That was when matters began getting very ugly for Birney and his abolitionists. From the *Carroll Free Press*:

At this juncture, however, the names of Birney, Donaldson, Colby and more [all leading abolitionists on the executive committee] were shouted by numerous voices and immediately three or four hundred of the mob rushed to Birney's dwelling. The mob were well provided with tar and feathers. On arriving at Birney's house, the abolition editor was demanded—his son, a youth of about sixteen, came to the door and assured the multitude that his father was not at home.

It was soon satisfactorily ascertained that he had left the city in the stage for Hillsboro [located just northeast of Sardinia] several hours previously. The mob then directed their course to the house of one of the Donaldsons (the other residing in the country) and demanded him to be delivered up to them. Some ladies came to the door, and pledged their word that Donaldson was not at home, and assured the multitude that no one but ladies were in the house. The mob immediately departed in search of, but did not succeed in finding him.

It was afterwards ascertained that he fled from the house a few minutes before the arrival of the mob, and had escaped through an alley or retired street to some unknown place. The cry of "Church alley" was now resounded through the mob. This is a place where a quantity of black and white men and women, of infamous characters reside, huddled promiscuously together in five or six small buildings.

In a few minutes the inmates of these wretched brothels were turned into the streets, and the windows of the buildings, and every article which the buildings contained [were] destroyed and scattered to the four winds of heaven.

Here by the peaceable interference of several citizens, the progress of the mob was arrested, (as was supposed, finally) everybody, apparently, promising to disperse and go home.

An hour or two afterwards, two or three hundred again collected together and demolished the windows and all the furniture of 6 or 7 small negro houses of bad character on and near the corner of Columbia and Elm Streets, in the part of the town commonly called the Swamp. In the course of this attack a gun was fired from the window of one of the houses, and a young man by the name of Kinsey was severely shot in the hip and leg with large sized pigeon shot. The wound we believe, is not considered very dangerous, though he was perforated with twenty-odd shot.

The mob having accomplished all they intended, finally dispersed about three o'clock on Sunday morning.

Some further movements occurred on Sunday night, caused by an impression that Birney was concealed in a house in Fourth Street. But a committee having examined the premises and reported that he was not there, the mob, after having been addressed by the mayor, dispersed. The city has since been quiet.

On the 2d of August a public meeting was called, which was addressed by Judge Burnet, Joseph Graham and Joseph S. Beham, Esqrs. After which resolutions were adopted pledging the meeting to support the civil authorities in their efforts to preserve the peace, and expressing an opinion that the recent outrages *were caused by the establishment of the abolition press.* [Emphasis, the author.]

Not reported in the article above was the fact Cincinnati mayor Samuel Davies actually participated in the riots and it was through his intervention the imbroglio ended.

Davies unashamedly offered up a midnight speech to the

beer-infused mob that included these words: "Gentleman—it is now late at night, and time we were all in bed—by continuing longer, you will disturb the citizens, or deprive them of their rest, besides robbing yourselves of rest. No doubt it is your intention to punish the guilty and leave the innocent. But if you continue longer, you are in danger of punishing the innocent with the guilty. We have done enough for one night. [Three cheers for the Mayor.] The Abolitionists themselves, must be convinced by this time, what public sentiment is, and that it will not do any longer to disregard or set it at naught. [Three cheers again.] As you cannot punish the guilty, without endangering the innocent, I advise you all to go home."

Mahan was shaken when hearing about the riot. He, Birney, and the rest of the executive committee had been co-founders of the Ohio Anti-Slavery Society just a year prior. Mahan had met Birney and many executive committee members. At the convention, he had eaten with them, prayed with and for them, and shared ideas. No one had expected this type of reckless lawlessness against the First Amendment to occur or else the Society wouldn't have ventured so soon into Cincinnati. Newspapers, local politicians, and law enforcement had all ganged up on them. Although having thousands of residents sympathetic to their cause, especially many Presbyterians, Cincinnati also had forty thousand people total, and many of them had anti-abolitionist beliefs and sympathies. The anti-abolitionists simply outnumbered and outgunned the abolitionists.

Mayor Samuel Davies and Cincinnati would have more race riots in 1841.

Setting the Stage: Sardinia & Southwest Ohio
CHAPTER TWO

The first white settler in Washington Township, in the area around present-day Sardinia in what is now Brown County, was Robert Wardlaw (spelled *Wardlow* by some descendants), this author's sixth-great grandfather, who settled two miles west of Sardinia, purchasing 1,002 acres in 1802, the year before Ohio became a state. He was a Presbyterian, and may have begun worshiping with other Presbyterians in that area early as 1808. According to family tradition, he had gone north out of Staunton, Virginia, to the free Northwest Territory because of his views against slavery, while most of his family—and their enslaved blacks—had moved from Virginia to South Carolina. The first Presbyterian church in that area began in 1811 two miles northeast of present-day Sardinia, in Highland County, on the road to Mowrystown.

A number of Methodist families settled about two miles southeast of Sardinia along Slab Camp Creek, where David Young, a Methodist circuit rider on the White Oak Circuit, began tending flock in 1808. The Methodists worshiped in homes and later, schoolhouses. The records of Methodist preachers serving from 1808 through 1820 are listed in *History of Brown County*, but none afterward, which would have been the same year (1820) John B. Mahan appeared in the Sardinia area. Many church records were lost due to a fire years later in nearby Mt. Orab, which had been part of the circuit. So, we don't know if John B. Mahan in 1820 was part of an official Methodist circuit, a Methodist "local preacher," or even Methodist. We do know he was nineteen. He had grown up Baptist.

John Bennington Mahan was born April 6, 1801, in Fleming County, Kentucky. His middle name was his mother's maiden name. His father Jacob was a Baptist pastor many years in Kentucky and moved with wife and children to present-day Clermont County in 1818. His father was against slavery. In the 1820s, he and his wife moved again, this time to Indiana, where he served as a Church of the United Brethren in Christ pastor and where Jacob most probably became the contact point between John B. Mahan and Levi Coffin, the famous Quaker abolitionist.

In 1828, Jacob volunteered as a missionary to an area in Wabash County, Indiana. He was John B. Mahan's role model in terms of faith, sacrificial living, and a determination to help others. John B. Mahan loved and respected his father. Mahan learned from his father how to be a shepherd to a flock. A Church of the United Brethren in Christ historian described Rev. Jacob Mahan and his fate:

> [He was] a large man, his manners were gentlemanly, and he was grave in his deportment. He possessed excellent conversational powers, and his sermons were clear, forcible and strong…[He] was then sent to the Wabash Mission. When on his way he stopped at my house, and during the conversation remarked that he never expected to return…He at once set out on horseback on his journey of two weeks through the cold and mud. He stopped near the Franklin Church and at Andersonville on his trip. After leaving Indianapolis he struck an Indian trail leading westward. In attempting to cross Sugar Creek, some miles below Crawfordsville, the swollen stream from heavy rains swept him off his horse that was swimming across. He lodged in a fallen tree top. After repeated calls he was extricated from his position by two

men who came to his rescue. He recovered his horse and succeeded in reaching his destination. He took cold from the exposure which later developed into serious lung trouble. However, he preached at his appointments, assisted in holding a camp meeting in which many were converted and organized a class of eleven members after which he was compelled to take his bed and after several weeks sickness he went to his eternal reward in January, 1829.

Hearing the way in which his father had perished (his mother certainly told him) and having a visual image on his heart and mind of his beloved father nearly drowning alone in a swollen river, one can imagine John B. Mahan having an overriding desire to help fugitive blacks in desperate need also trying to cross a dangerous river.

John B. Mahan settled in Perry Township, in northernmost Brown County about 1820, not far from his parents who were then still in Clermont County and not yet in Indiana. Later that same year in Brown County, Mahan married Polly (also called Mary) Stairs on December 19. As we know from Birney, Mahan, by that time, already had been helping fugitive blacks flee southern slavery.

Years later, it would seem he and a younger brother, William, moved with their wives to Highland County, Ohio, on Bell's Run, a small stream that joins White Oak Creek northeast of Sardinia. (Sardinia sits on the extreme northern edge of Brown County, straddling the Highland County line.) John later moved to Brown County. Mahan, in various documents, has been described as a farmer, school teacher, preacher, inn owner, saw mill operator, grist mill operator, township fence viewer (1836-38), and township overseer of the poor (1839-42). Like many settlers, he likely did what he had to do to feed his family.

In about 1831, he and John Dunham built a saw mill and a grist mill, on Slab Camp Creek southeast of Sardinia, and operated the mills until a dam needed for water power failed in 1834-35. That ended the milling businesses. About that same time Mahan opened a "Temperance Tavern," a business that did not serve alcohol and acted as a travelers' inn. He probably viewed his losing the saw mill as God simply redirecting his path for something better.

The mid-1830s were chaotic, stressful, and yet exciting for Mahan and his family. He was trying to raise a family, survive a business failure, and earn a decent living. He also had to emotionally deal with the death of his mother Martha, who had moved to Sardinia after her husband died in Indiana. She passed away in Sardinia and was buried there in 1834. According to the Census, Martha was not living with either of her sons in 1830, John or William, so she likely moved there soon after the Census. Her death weighed heavily on John's heart. (John B. Mahan eventually was buried next to his mother in Sardinia Cemetery.)

The year 1834 was when, according to Dr. Isaac Beck, the Underground Railroad began operating in Sardinia, which, for the first few years, at least, involved Sardinia as the first "whistle" stop north of Ripley. Mahan already had been helping fugitive blacks on his own. He had the real fear, given federal fugitive slave laws, that the very people he was trying to help could be caught and pirated back to Kentucky, or that he himself could be convicted or murdered by Kentucky slave hunters, who had the impolite habit at all hours of pounding loudly on doors in Sardinia looking for "property."

The Mahan clan grew. The 1830 U.S. Census listed John's family as having one male under age five, one male between twenty and thirty (John), one female under five, and two females between ages five and ten. Polly was listed as being between twenty and thirty, for a total of six family members. (The 1840 Census noted ten family members.)

The first two homes built in Sardinia, in 1831, were that of Dr. Isaac Beck and Josiah Moore, both of whom joined Mahan in becoming abolitionists. Mahan probably built Beck's home for him and used wood cut at Mahan's sawmill. (Both houses still stand today at 125 and 126 North Main.)

In 1892, in a letter, Dr. Isaac Beck identified Mahan as a "Methodist local preacher," which in Methodist Episcopal Church jargon meant he was a lay person who had been given authority by his denomination to preach, lead worship, and assist circuit rider preachers in discipling a particular congregation. Perhaps use of the term "Reverend" in our day and age for Mahan would be too generous. He was not seminary trained. Two kinds of "local" Methodist Episcopal preachers existed: those who had been on circuit but found as a circuit rider they could no longer support a family, and thus became "localized"; and others who had been given a license to preach even though they had never been on circuit.

Given John B. Mahan's (and his brother's) purchase of farm land in the Sardinia area, his work history of owning a saw mill and a grist mill, and of teaching school, and of his having a young family to feed, and the fact no records exist of him being a circuit rider, it would seem he was never a circuit rider but more in the mold of a "local preacher" licensed to preach and lead worship.

One sign he wasn't a "full" minister: He did not self-identify as "Reverend" Mahan at the Ohio Anti-Slavery Convention in 1835, only as John B. Mahan, while Rankin was listed as Rev. John Rankin.

A number of early Methodist families settled near Slab Camp Creek in Washington Township, about two miles southeast of present-day Sardinia, first meeting at the home of Andrew Nevin, and later at schoolhouses. Methodist circuit riders on the White Oak Circuit began visiting in 1808, with services held in or near Slab Camp Creek until after 1850, when the church built on property in town. Slab Camp Creek most probably was where Mahan served as a Methodist local preacher. He took his spiritual work seriously, just like his father had.

Erastus Mahan, John's nephew, while relating part of a story he had heard from John's wife, Polly, who later lived near him in Illinois for years after John's death, wrote in 1899:

> My father, and his older brother, John Bennington Mahan, married sisters, Cassandra and Mary [Polly] Curtis, and settled on the same quarter section of land, on a little stream called Bell's Run, in the southern part of Highland County, Ohio. A few years afterward my father became the sole owner of the 160 acres of land and his brother, John B., moved into Brown County, about three miles from my father's home and settled on a stream called White Oak where he, in connection with others, located the town of Sardinia.

The United States at that time had a number of social movements that had arisen out of the Second Great Awakening., i.e., the spiritual revival that started in camp meetings in Kentucky around 1800 before spreading nationwide, with the most notable being the Cane Ridge Camp Meeting that occurred near Paris, Kentucky. Twenty thousand Kentuckians had attended Cane Ridge. The "temperance" and "anti-slavery" movements of the 1830s had arisen from the revivals—and they were gaining steam nationally.

John B. Mahan, and friend, Dr. Isaac Beck, were early activists for both. For example, Mahan built a "Temperance Tavern" in 1835 (no alcohol allowed), a business which also served as an inn, with the building still standing (2025) at Sardinia's main intersection. Dr. Beck delivered his first temperance lecture August 1, 1830, in what was one of Ohio's first lay temperance lectures.

No doubt, the stunning successes seen regarding Americans embracing alcohol abstinence across vast swaths of the nation (including Ohio) must have fueled on similar dreams and hopes for Mahan, Beck, and others, regarding Ohio abolitionist efforts. The temperance and abolitionist movements often were joined at the hip. In their eyes, they were trying to help people get free from sin, i.e., the sins of alcohol abuse and slavery. An editorial from *The Troy (Ohio) Times* read, for instance: [Note: Newspapers then often called abolition advocates "philanthropists."]

> The philanthropist, the real lover of his race, cannot contemplate but with joy the extraordinary change that has taken place in almost every section of our Republic, in relation to the cause of temperance. Some thirty years ago, the most rigid church disciplinarian did not place the same restrictions upon his appetite; neither did that severe censure rest upon an erring brother that now awaits the indulgence in ardent spirits. The moral sense of the

people has undergone a striking change: Distilleries have vanished and school houses and churches occupy their places. Where the bottle and vulgar song, and boisterous mirth freely circulated, we now have rational conversation—hymns of praise, and a sober interchange of sentiment. The bloated inebriate has given place to the sober citizen; dilapidated houses and filthy tenements have disappeared, and handsome houses and comfortable cottages erected in their stead: heartbroken wives have obliterated their sorrows, and the once ragged and ignorant children being to appear decently clad, and exhibit evidences of good breeding; farms that had gone to waste, fields overrun with briars and weeds, fences broken down and everything in a state of decay and ruin, are now in high cultivation and in ample order.

One would naturally be led to enquire what has produced this wonderful revolution—what has brought about so happy a change in all these things—what has transformed this desolate wilderness, this barren waste to fruitful fields and flowery meads? It is the successful efforts of those who embarked and have struggled in the cause of Temperance...Let no one despise temperance societies, nor point a scoffing finger to its members; great has been the good resulting to the human family through their agencies, and more will yet be accomplished: God has blessed the work, and what He deigns to bless will prosper.

As a Methodist local preacher, Mahan most certainly was involved in serving, evangelizing, and discipling the free black Gist Settlement. The Settlement was relatively close (within a mile) to the Methodist settlers at Slab Camp Creek, and only three miles east of Sardinia.

Samuel Gist, a wealthy English land owner, had vast

Virginia plantations, yet had never set foot once on American soil to survey his investments. In his last will and testament, after providing large sums to his only daughter, Mary, he left the rest of his wealth at his 1815 death to his more than one thousand Virginia enslaved blacks—people he had never met—and declared they "shall be free." Gist wanted his Virginia plantations sold, "comfortable" homes purchased for his slaves, and school houses and churches built for them—in a *free state*. He set aside up to fifty pounds annually for a Protestant pastor to "teach the Christian religion." After several years of delay involving the reticent Virginia executrix, Mary, Gist's daughter, two tracts of Brown County land eventually were located, including a tract in Eagle Township, which bordered Washington Township, near present-day Sardinia. The estate trustees inked the deal on November 17, 1819.

Gist's free blacks inherited land covered with tangled undergrowth and marshland that was unfit for farming, let alone living. But they came anyway to Brown County. The very first of several Gist settlements began near Sardinia in 1820. Almost five hundred settlers arrived, with up to fifty families eventually calling Eagle Township home. Other Gist families ended up later near Georgetown, which was the county seat when Brown County was carved out of Clermont County in 1818. (There were other Ohio Gist locations outside Brown County.)

Contrary to instructions in Gist's will, the executrix or trustees failed to build schoolhouses or churches for the former slaves. They had poor farm land. The estate executors did not do their job well—maybe on purpose. The 1820s was a difficult decade for these newly freed blacks. Some probably wished they hadn't been freed. Some returned to Virginia. The Gist settlers eventually would become embroiled in lawsuits among themselves over property and land, and disreputable whites tried cheating them.

That said, the community had some positive outcomes and they did what they could to survive. By 1835, the Sardinia "Camp" of Gist settlers had dwindled to three hundred and fifty. A school existed for about eight months in 1834, a "Gist" temperance society had thirty members, and both had the signature of John B. Mahan written all over it.

At the 1835 Ohio Anti-Slavery Society convention, a committee named "Condition of People of Color" offered a report on the Sardinia Gist settlement, with information that had to have been provided by Sardinians Abraham Pettijohn and John B. Mahan.

> Notwithstanding this, we find among this (Sardinia Gist) people a latent intellect, not a whit behind that of white citizens, a docility and readiness to be benefitted which invites effort in their behalf, and a state of morals, discouraging indeed to those who look to mere human agency to correct and elevate; but full of the highest stimulus to those whose confidence is in God and the power of his gospel.

The free blacks in the Gist Settlement provided an ally and "cover" for the work of John B. Mahan and Sardinia abolitionists. These hundreds of blacks who had only recently been freed from slavery themselves, and having a natural empathy towards fellow blacks trying to flee, and residing but three miles away, would prove pivotal to the success of Mahan's stop on the Underground Railroad, particularly a Gist settler named John Hudson.

Free Ohio blacks, like Hudson, had to be extremely careful, always taking precautions to avoid being around the presence of unscrupulous Kentuckians with the habit of abducting free Ohio blacks and selling them to Kentucky slave masters. Thievery paid well.

Such was the case with thirty-two-year-old Eliza Jane Johnson, a free black woman who had lived in Ripley three years before being abducted and forced across the Ohio River to Mason County, Kentucky. Legally, Kentucky considered every black a slave until proven otherwise by their "free papers." Though Johnson's supposed slave owner admitted her abduction had been a mistake—she just looked like his fugitive slave—the Mason County sheriff continued holding her after hearing she had been under slavery years earlier in New Orleans. Given she was black, and presumed a slave, she could not testify on her own behalf.

While Johnson wrung hands and wept in her jail cell and felt abandoned, her husband and friends in Ripley feared for her life. By Kentucky law, given her race, and the assumption she was a fugitive, the sheriff had the legal right to keep her in jail while running newspaper ads for her supposed master to claim her. This could go on for up to a year, and if no slave owner claimed her, the county sheriff could sell her into slavery to recoup the costs of incarceration.

Rev. Rankin and others visited Mason County court to lobby for Eliza Jane Johnson and while there vowed to lobby Ohio Governor Vance and the Ohio state legislature for her release. (Thankfully, as you will learn, Mahan did not join Rankin on this mission of mercy to Kentucky.)

While the abolitionists rode horseback home to Ohio without Johnson, a Sardinian, James Huggins, who had been riding ahead of the others, was attacked by anti-abolitionists, stripped, tied to a tree, and viciously whipped.

Democrat U.S. Senator Thomas Morris of Ohio, an abolitionist and uncle of Dr. Isaac Beck, was livid upon hearing the news. A Kentucky newspaper reported him as allegedly saying that "war ought to be immediately declared against Kentucky and that every Kentuckian should be shot down so soon as he set his foot on the Ohio side."

It literally took an act of the Ohio Legislature to get Eliza Jane Johnson free. On March 9, 1838, the Legislature passed the following resolution: "Whereas, It is represented to this General Assembly that Eliza Jane Johnson, a free woman of color, was lately carried by force, and without legal authority, from her home in Brown County, Ohio, into Mason County, Kentucky, on the pretense of being a slave of Arthur Fox, of said county of Mason, and though the said Arthur Fox disclaims any title to said Eliza, she is still detained in confinement in the jail of said county: Therefore, Resolved, That his Excellency the Governor be, and he is hereby requested to open a correspondence with the Governor of Kentucky, in relation to the illegal seizure and forcible removal of said Eliza Jane Johnson, from Brown County, Ohio, to Mason County, Kentucky, where she is detained in prison, and that he respectfully insists on the restoration of said Eliza Jane Johnson to the enjoyment of freedom and friends."

The world outside Sardinia was rapidly changing, including the recent invention of steam engine trains out East—and Mahan could see Ohio culture rapidly changing, too. Perhaps he would not have to wait long for slave hunters to stop pounding on his door.

For example, American abolitionists were thrilled hearing the incredible news that the British Parliament in 1833 had outlawed slavery everywhere in the British Empire. (The Act became effective August 1834.)

Former U.S. President John Quincy Adams, now a congressman, was a champion of the abolitionist cause in the U.S. House of Representatives.

Lane Seminary (Presbyterian) in Cincinnati held major "debates" in 1834—really more forums for differing anti-slavery voices. The guest list included a Who's Who of abolitionists, including James G. Birney, Rev. John Rankin, Harriet Beecher Stowe, Asa Mahan (later Oberlin College president, no relation to John B.), and Theodore Weld, debate organizer. These debates pre-dated two years the Cincinnati Riots and its success may have led abolitionists later to overestimate Cincinnati abolitionist sentiment.

Mahan may have been present at the Lane Debates, but if not, in the least he heard about what had been presented from friend Rev. John Rankin, or from numerous newspaper accounts. He had never felt so excited.

The debates ran forty-five hours over nine days and entertained but two questions: Should slave-holding states abolish slavery immediately? and; Are the doctrines, tendencies, and measures of the American Colonization Society, and the influence of its principal supports, such as render it worthy of the patronage of the Christian public? (The American Colonization Society encouraged free blacks to move to Liberia. The debates were between Colonization Society members and Abolitionists.)

The debate atmosphere was electric and eclectic, to say the least. The star ended up being an emancipated slave, James Bradley, the only black debater. He won hearts and minds. A speaker prior to Bradley had remarked, and the audience had just concurred, that "blacks are abundantly able to take care of, and provide for themselves; and that they would be kind and docile if immediately emancipated." The commentary by an observer:

> James Bradley...addressed us nearly two hours; and I wish his speech could have been heard by every opponent of immediate emancipation, to wit: first that it would be unsafe to the community"; second, that "the condition of the emancipated negroes would be worse than it now is; that they are incompetent to provide for themselves; that they would become paupers and vagrants, and would rather steal than work for wages."

> This shrewd and intelligent black, cut up these *white objections* by their roots, and withered and scorched them under the sun of sarcastic argumentation, for nearly an hour, to which the assembly responded in repeated and spontaneous roars of laughter, which were heartily joined in by both Colonizationists and Abolitionists. Do not understand me as saying, that his speech was devoid of *argument*. No. It contained sound logic, enforced by apt illustrations. I wish the slanderers of negro intellect could have witnessed this unpremeditated effort.

> I will give you a sketch of this man's history. He was stolen from Africa when an infant, and sold into slavery. His master, who resided in Arkansas, died, leaving him to his widow. He was then about eighteen years of age. For some years, *he managed the plantation for his mistress.* Finally, he purchased his time by the year, and began to earn money to buy his freedom. After five years of toil, having paid his owners $655, besides supporting himself during the time, he received his "free papers," and emigrated to a free State with more than $200 in his pocket. Every cent

of this money, $855 (total), he earned by labor and trading. He is now a beloved and respected member of this institution (Lane Seminary).

No, Mr. Editor, can slaves take care of themselves if emancipated? I answer the question in the language employed by brother Bradley, on the above occasion. "They have to take care of, and support themselves *now, and their master, and his family into the bargain*; and this being so, it would be strange if they could not provide for themselves, *when disencumbered from this load*."

Using the Lane Seminary debates as a catalyst, more than a hundred Ohio abolitionists, including Birney and Mahan, joined to inaugurate the Ohio Anti-Slavery Society at Zanesville from April 22-25, 1835. Theirs was a branch of the American Anti-Slavery Society. It was a seminal moment for Ohio abolitionists and created kindling for more abolitionist sentiment statewide—perhaps more so than the Lane Seminary debates.

Six Brown Countians arrived as delegates at the first convention: John B. Mahan, Nathan Galbraith, Rev. John Rankin, Rev. Robert Rutherford, Stephen Riggs, and fellow Sardinian, Abraham Pettijohn. The convention's first official "declaration of sentiment" made crystal clear to Ohioans that theirs was a holy war. It set the tone. The "declaration of sentiment" below is printed in its entirety. Twenty-two of one hundred eleven delegates were Christian ministers, who wore their Christian abolitionist beliefs on their sleeves for Ohio newspaper editors to testify about, including those in Cincinnati.

> We believe Slavery to be a sin—always, everywhere and only sin. Sin in itself, apart from the occasional rigors

incidental to its administration and from all those perils, liabilities, and positive inflictions to which its victims are continually exposed, sin in the nature of the act which creates it, and in the elements which constitute it. Sin, because it converts persons into things; makes men property, God's image, merchandise. Because it forbids men to use themselves for the advancement of their own well-being, and turns them into mere instruments to be used by others solely for the benefit of the users. Because it constitutes one man the owner of the body, soul and spirit of other men—gives him power and permission to make his own pecuniary profit the great end of their being, thus striking them out of existence as beings possessing rights and susceptibilities of happiness, and forcing them to exist merely as appendages to his own existence.

In other words, because slavery *holds and uses men, as mere means for the accomplishment of ends, of which ends their own interests are not a part*—thus annihilating the sacred and eternal distinction between a person and a thing, a distinction proclaimed an axiom by all human consciousness—a distinction created by God—crowned with glory and honor in the attributes of intelligence, morality, accountability and immortal existence and commended to the homage of universal mind, by the concurrent testimony of nature, conscience, providence and revelation, by the blood of atonement and the sanctions of eternity, authenticated by the seal of Deity and in its own nature, effaceless and immutable.

This distinction slavery contemns, disannuls and tramples under foot. This is its fundamental element—its vital constituent principle, that which makes it a *sin in itself* under whatever modification existing. All the incidental effects of the system flow spontaneously from this fountain-head. The constant exposure of slaves to outrage and the actual inflictions which they experience in innumerable forms, all result legitimately from this principle, assumed in the theory and embodied in the practice of slave holding.

  What is that but a SIN which sinks to the level of brutes, beings ranked and registered by God a little lower than the angels—wrests from their rightful owners the legacies which their maker has bequeathed them—inalienable birthright endowments exchanged for no equivalent, unsurrendered by volition and unforfeited by crime—breaks open the sanctuary of human rights and makes its sacred things common plunder, driving to the shambles Jehovah's image, herded with four footed beasts and creeping things, and bartering for vile dust the purchase of a Redeemer's blood, and the living members of his body? What is that but a sin, which derides the sanctity with which God has invested domestic relations, annihilates marriage, makes void parental authority, nullifies filial obligation, invites the violation of chastity by denying it legal protection, thus bidding God speed to lust at riots at noon-day, glorying in the immunities of law? What is that but a sin which stamps as crime obedience to the command "search the Scriptures," repeals the law of love, abrogates the golden rule, exacts labor without recompense, authorizes the forcible sunderings of kindred and cut off forever from the pursuit of happiness?—What is that but a sin which embargoes the acquisition of knowledge by the terror of penalties, eclipses intellect, stifles the native instincts of the heart, precipitates in death damps the upward aspirations of the spirit, startles its victims with present perils, peoples the future with apprehended horrors, palsies the moral sense, whelms hope in despair and kills the soul?

The name and reputation of John B. Mahan already carried some gravitas: the first official act of the convention chair was to appoint a six-member committee to nominate officers. John B. Mahan was appointed, as was Theodore Weld, who had organized the Lane Seminary Debates.

The assembly also appointed Mahan to a seven-man "resolutions" committee, which included James G. Birney. Outside of the people he knew through Rankin, Mahan suddenly was moving in fast abolitionist circles of which he had never before been part, and spending quality time with many of these men, getting to know their families, lives, and passions, and learning whom he could trust. At times, he couldn't believe he was working alongside abolitionists he had only read about. He viewed this as God's blessing.

This resolutions committee adopted nineteen resolutions in all, including ones recognizing the plight of female slaves, the importance of Christianizing Africa, the lack of a need to transport enslaved blacks to Africa for their "highest happiness," condemning free-state whites who went South to own slaves, believing the sin of slavery rested on the members of God's visible church, condemning slave-holding among Christians, castigating slave owners for withholding Bible learning and education, and calling for the Christian Church universal to hold a "concert of prayer" the last Monday of every month on behalf of enslaved and free people of color.

After eyeing a document calling for members to be "solemnly consecrated to the cause of Emancipation, Immediate, Total, and Universal," Mahan boldly signed in cursive his name right after Abraham Pettijohn and Theodore Weld. (He may have taken a few seconds beforehand to realize he could be signing his own death warrant, just as several Declaration of Independence signers had done.)

Article Two of their anti-slavery society constitution read, "The object of the Society shall be the entire abolition of Slavery throughout the United States, and the elevation of our colored brethren to their proper rank as men."

Mahan was named "Manager" of the Ohio Anti-Slavery Society for all of Brown County. His important role in the Society was now made public for the whole world to see: even for Kentucky slave owners and hunters.

Mahan listened as convention speakers made animated speeches, and reported on the conditions of "free colored people of Ohio," repressive Ohio laws affecting free blacks, establishment of a newspaper that would be called *The Philanthropist*, the American slave trade, a resolution to abolish the Washington D.C. slave trade, the appointment of delegates to the American Anti-Slavery Society convention, endorsement letters from supporters who could not attend.

While horseback riding the one hundred twenty-five-mile trip home from Zanesville to Sardinia along with Abraham Pettijohn, John Rankin, and others, Mahan's thoughts spun and spun trying to process all the information, the palpable excitement, the connections made, the warm spirit. His own spirit felt emboldened discovering so many men of like mind. His resolve had been hardened.

On that way home, protesters attacked Rankin and the Brown Countians several times, pelting them with stones and eggs, once after Rankin preached at a black church.

Mahan's thoughts continued spinning throughout 1835 as abolition talk spilled out all over the nation, like a mighty churning river overflowing its banks and spreading into low-lying farm fields. Literally within a week after Mahan returned from the state convention, the American Anti-Slavery Society in New York City began mailing out what would eventually be a million pieces of anti-slavery literature directly into homes nationwide, including those in the South. The vast mailing, once received, triggered a severe backlash, including thefts and public burnings of mail bags containing abolitionist literature, anti-abolitionist meetings and parades throughout the South, boycotting products, the harassing of abolitionists, and more death threats and bounties than could be counted. The latter was primarily aimed at Arthur Tappan, American Anti-Slavery Society co-founder. (Ironically, his brother Benjamin Tappan became an anti-abolitionist Ohio U.S. Senator.) The number of anti-slavery societies nationwide nearly tripled. It seemed Ohio was fertile ground for abolitionist growth, too. It was as if abolitionists were turning the world upside-down by using the 1830s equivalent of a modern direct mail campaign.

In 1836, the cause spread and Ohio Anti-Slavery Societies began popping up in cities throughout Southwest Ohio, in part because Rankin had taken six months off to be a traveling preacher/presenter for the American Anti-Slavery Society. The first church he spoke at was in Mowrystown, the first town north of Sardinia. It was a strategic move in terms of developing helpers for Mahan. Rankin preached at Goshen, Williamsburg, New Richmond, West Union, Winchester, Withamsville, Decatur. Wherever he went, he found people interested in starting a local anti-slavery society.

Rankin often encountered stiff resistance traveling the Southwest Ohio countryside. Then the 1836 Cincinnati Riots broke out, anti-abolitionist protesters wrecked *The Philanthropist*, and the *terra firma* below Mahan's feet quaked.

You could see Mahan's smile widening though. Abolitionists obviously had been having a profound effect. The consciences of Americans all over were being pricked, one by one, a process that had to occur before any lasting political or social change.

Setting the Stage: The People
CHAPTER THREE

In the course of writing a biography, sometimes an author can get tunnel vision focusing solely on the person of interest. But much of John B. Mahan's story also involved the actual real Sardinians who helped him, and the black fugitives he guided on the Underground Railroad on their flight north.

Other than statements about the one fugitive black directly involved in the incident leading to three of John B. Mahan's four trials, only perhaps a dozen accounts exist of interactions with fugitives stopping in Sardinia or a couple dozen or more about their Sardinia helpers who were involved on the Railroad.

As for Sardinians, we do know something about Josiah Moore, who settled Sardinia in the early 1830s and who, along with Dr. Beck, each owned one of the village's first two homes. (It was Josiah's father, John, who "molded" the early community ethos. He was a Presbyterian Church elder from 1812 to when the church became Congregational in 1851.) Son Josiah Moore was well-liked in the community, quite bright, active in the Presbyterian Church in Sardinia, and had "splendid social qualities." In 1843, the Free Soil Party named him to run as its Brown County representative. He lost. Like Beck, and Mahan, he was a temperance advocate.

By 1829, Sardinia had at least a dozen Pettijohn families, and they all had abolitionist sympathies, including the family of Amos, who was a Presbyterian elder. A number of Pettijohns later became physicians.

David Graham was a founding member of White Oak

Presbyterian Church, and his daughter married Dr. Isaac Beck.

We know much about Beck. His contributions to the Underground Railroad in Sardinia cannot be overstated and not just because his maternal uncle was Ohio Democratic U.S. Senator Thomas Morris, the senator at the time of Mahan's first trial. Morris was Ohio's best-known political supporter of abolition. With Morris as a helper, Dr. Beck and Mahan indirectly had connections to political power in Columbus and Washington. Morris would become an abolitionist mouthpiece, and in 1844 he ran as the vice-presidential candidate under James G. Birney on the nationwide anti-slavery Liberty Party ticket.

Beck's first job at age seventeen was working for six months in 1824 in Georgetown, the Brown County seat, for Thomas L. Hamer, owner of *The Benefactor* newspaper, and who later would serve as Fifth District U.S. Congressman. Hamer was fiercely anti-abolitionist (as Mahan would learn on September 17, 1838) and would become one of Mahan and Beck's bitterest enemies. Beck *knew* what made this man tick. Beck soon switched his interest away from printing, studied, and earned at age twenty-one a license to practice medicine. In 1829, he relocated to where the town of Sardinia would start and he and his wife would rear eight children there. Eventually, he would be buried in Sardinia Cemetery. It was Mahan who probably built Beck's home for him.

At his own admission, Beck began working on the Underground Railroad about 1835, around the time of the forming of the Ohio Anti-Slavery Society, back when Beck was still a Jackson Democrat. Over time he would change political parties depending on which party was most pro-abolitionist: first, the Whig Party in 1838, Liberty Party in 1840, Free Soil Party in 1848, and finally, the Republican Party, in 1856.

Along the way, he was also a "temperance" man, of course, giving his first lecture against alcohol in 1830 to a Methodist Episcopal audience in Highland County and fifty years later speaking on the same topic. Here are his own words about his life.

> My father was one of the Kentucky Emancipation Baptists that agitated and divided the Baptist Church in that State about the commencement of the present century. Hence, hatred of slavery was one of the earliest sentiments impressed on my mind. But the organization and agitation of the American Colonization Society demoralized me with thousands of others and I became infatuated with the doctrine of "gradual emancipation."
> When the Abolitionists came preaching immediate emancipation, I opposed them earnestly but I soon found I could not logically oppose the Abolitionists without justifying slavery and that my conscience would not permit (it), and hence I became an Abolitionist and an "Underground Railroader" in 1835....I opposed slavery as long as it existed, and expect to oppose moderate and immoderate drinking as long as I exist....So to religion I first united with the Baptist Church, but after two or three years I became a Christian [Disciple for] nearly fifty years since and yet so remain nor do I anticipate any further change in that. I preached [as a pastor in that denomination] three or four years, until I preached away a pretty good practice, and nearly all I had accumulated by my practice in fifteen years. I then concluded I had done my share. I had a family to feed. I was an abolitionist and Teetotaler. Both were unprofitable

in those days.

Fortunately for historians, in 1892, then 85-year-old Dr. Isaac Beck wrote a letter (a part of which you just read) that also chronicled his memories of twenty-two years spent on the Underground Railroad in Sardinia. His information has been invaluable in terms of historians learning certain Brown County origins of the Underground Railroad, the names of co-workers and specific incidents in Sardinia, his personal views regarding what happened at Mahan's trials, and preserving stories about blacks fleeing slavery.

As for others helping Mahan on the Underground Railroad, in the towns around Sardinia, was a group of Southwest Ohio pastors putting their lives, livelihoods, and church members' lives on the line fighting for abolition. In terms of actual pastors involved, at first, they mostly were in the Chillicothe Presbytery of the Presbyterian Church, with nearly all the pastors having been Southern men who had voluntarily vacated slave states for free soil Ohio. They hated slavery.

This group of abolitionist Presbyterian pastors (who would soon experience a denominational split, in part because of slavery) included Rankin of Ripley, Gilliland of Red Oak, Lockhart of Russellville, Dobbins of Sardinia (who would soon leave for Illinois), Corothers and Steele of next-door Highland County, and Burgess, who would lead the Sardinia church (White Oak Presbyterian) at least three different times. Presbyterian churches in rural Southwest Ohio became what could be called abolitionist cells—they, along with a few other churches, including Quaker and Methodist, and others smitten by the cause.

If John Rankin was the "Father" of Brown County abolition, James Gilliland could be called the "Grandfather." Born 1769 in South Carolina, Gilliland began preaching against "the sin of slavery" in 1796 after his ordination. The Presbytery of South Carolina ordered him "to be silent in the pulpit on the subject of the emancipation of the Africans," to which he abided, only to privately start teaching abolition. He followed his presbytery order until 1804-05 when he no longer complied and found a like-minded Brown County church in need of a pastor. Gilliland's Red Oak Presbyterian founded four other Brown County Presbyterian churches: Ripley, Decatur, Russellville, and Georgetown. Literally, Gilliland started preaching abolition in Brown County the same year William Lloyd Garrison was born and when Mahan was only four.

For these pastors involved with Mahan, the abolitionist fervor arrived full-force January 1, 1831, like a yellow sun beam of hope slicing through abject darkness, with the publishing, reading, and sharing of *The Liberator*, a Boston abolitionist newspaper published by this same William Lloyd Garrison, co-founder of the American Anti-Slavery Society. The newspaper would become a source of information for a nation, influencing Rankin, Mahan, and all who worked with them, including free blacks.

The Liberator's first major news coverage occurred in August that year, when Nat Turner spawned a slave revolt in Virginia that took the lives of more than fifty whites. *The Liberator* re-published articles from Virginia newspapers, particularly about the bloodless capture of Turner, who confessed his crime.

Again, the particular Underground Railroad line running through and near Sardinia was not the good work of just one man, John B. Mahan, or even of a few helpers, such as Dr. Beck, Josiah Moore, and Abraham Pettijohn, or pastors, but was a community effort. Mahan, within just a few miles of Sardinia, could count on the support of a dozen Huggins men, four Kincaids, four Moores, four Grahams, John Mahan's brother William, two Pangburns, S.W. Gilliland, William Frazier, and A.B. Crane, not to mention a slew of Pettijohns and Dr. Beck. Add to that their wives and children. Theirs was a tight-knit abolitionist community focused on a Christian goal of loving blacks as neighbors, not as property. Mahan was thankful for every one of his neighbors, and knew he could not do his work without their help.

The Sardinia portion of this particular Underground Railroad line wasn't officially organized, meaning it didn't have a constitution, elected officers or bylaws. But it had rules—the Golden Rule, said Beck, and the rule that every man did what "seemed right in his own eyes" at a particular moment. You could say being an abolitionist was shoot from the hip, and had to be.

Possibly the Sardinian guiding more fugitives than anyone north towards Canada wasn't white, but John Hudson, a free black from the Gist Settlement, who Beck said was smart and had obtained, on his own, an education as "good as our common laborers." (In part, that education probably came from Mahan.) Hudson had a well-built, massive frame, and when riled up had "no more fear than a mad bull." Sardinian abolitionists paid Hudson a fair wage for time lost at work while guiding fugitives up the line.

Sardinians, like Hudson, usually accompanied fugitives

on foot at night, but sometimes in a wagon or on horseback, depending on situation, time of day, and weather conditions. The fugitives usually arrived alone or in twos, but sometimes came in larger groups, including once, twelve. The specific route from Sardinia was determined in a similar spontaneous fashion, but more often than not on where Kentucky slave hunters had been searching and whether they were in close pursuit.

Sardinia activity on "The Road" lasted from 1834 to 1856, when the creation of the Republican Party galvanized so much pro-abolitionist sentiment that nearly "every Republican became a Railroader," said Beck.

He and other abolitionists were hampered most in their work during the long four years the Ohio Fugitive Slave Law of 1839 existed—covering roughly the same time frame in which Mahan faced his four trials—when abolitionist peer-to-peer communication slowed and the network became far more cautious in order to avoid suspicion and the attention of the Brown County sheriff. Sardinians did what they could to help fugitives during this trying period.

Here are a number of stories, mildly edited for clarity and printed in their entirety, that Beck shared about real Sardinians, and the real fugitives they helped escape over a more than twenty-year period.

> Previous to [1834], occasionally a slave would cross the river on his way to Canada, but no person felt much interest in him anyway, either to help or hinder him if he was hungry. They would feed him—(and) if he inquired, they would tell him the road (to go on). But when [Ohioans] learned that the practice of slavery was unjust oppression, and sinful, they thought like Paul, "If thou mayest be free use it rather" and if it was right for a slave

to run off it was right to help him, if he needed help, and they remembered the Golden Rule.

When a fugitive would cross the river, they were very likely to hear of these abolitionists or the [Gist Camps such as near Sardinia] and endeavor to find them. Then they were helped to our neighborhood, for the colored people (at Gist Settlement) thought [the fugitive] safer among the whites than with themselves—and they were right, for the slave hunters would be more apt to use violence on them than on whites.

When [the fugitives came] here, at first, we sent them to Colonel Keys in Hillsboro, Ohio, or to John Nelson four miles east of that place, and generally they, I think, sent them to the brothers Rodgers near Greenfield, Ohio. At a later period, we sometimes sent them to Thomas Hobson in Wilmington, but that being forty miles was too long for a night's travel. We shortened it by finding help among a large neighborhood of Quakers at Martinsville. The principal depot was at Aaron Betts, a wealthy Quaker. We then shortened this again by finding David Sewal and the Bales Wesleyan Methodists, two miles beyond Lynchburg.

Afterward we found another route east of here to John McClanahan's four miles north of Winchester in Adams County.

We operated differently from other Railroads. Our aim was safety not speed, for it made little difference to the fugitive whether he was a week or a month in getting to Canada so that he got there safely and was fed on the way.

Among the first fugitives I saw were two men about thirty years old who said they had come from Tennessee. They had been sold to a trader [and were] to be taken South and hired out to work in harvest, [and the master] bought them to complete the "gang." For safety, at night they were handcuffed, fettered and chained to the floor in a cabin. In the morning, they were unfettered and taken to the field to cradle wheat with their handcuffs on. A hatchet was given them to fix their cradles.

One night, they managed to get the hatchet into the cabin, and with the hatchet, succeeded in freeing themselves from the floor. They escaped to the woods where, with the hatchet, they released themselves from the fetters and handcuffs. One's courage failed and he went back, but the other two started North, traveling as best they could, reaching Ohio in twenty-one days living on green apples and blackberries, except one meal.

Arriving one Sunday morning at a small secluded farm, they were so near famished they concluded they must have food. They found a position in the woods, where they had a good view of a house, then waited until they were satisfied that the only persons about it were an old man and woman…The dog barked, and the man came out. They frankly confessed [to be] fugitives and nearly starved. He invited them in. The old lady provided a meal part of which consisted of a large uncut "Pone" of corn bread. They ate and when about to leave the old gentleman gave them the remainder of the pone to take with them, which was all they ate, except blackberries and green apples, for twenty-one days. When I saw them, the scabs were still on the sores on their wrists, worn by the handcuffs while cradling grain.

William Taylor of Mason County, Kentucky, had a slave he called Ike who made a start for Canada, [and] by some means [Ike] arrived at the Negro settlement near Sardinia and tarried a few days. A [white] man of the basest sort, who had recently moved to a farm in the vicinity with the assistance of others of the same sort, arrested Ike and, probably thinking they could negotiate with Taylor for the reward on better terms on their ground than on his, sent a messenger with the news of Ike's capture.

Taylor returned with the messenger but arrived too late in the day to start back with him. Late in the evening Taylor, Ike, and his captors were sitting on the porch and a goodly number of the Camp negroes were loafing around, among them John Hudson. Taylor and his friends were invited in to supper. When they obeyed the invitation, Ike, who was under guard, went in with them. When Taylor saw Ike, he ordered him out of the room.

Ike obeyed and left the room, but forgot to stop on the porch. It was but a short distance to the woods and one of the loafing negroes assumed the office of guide. When the captors learned of Ike's treachery, they started in pursuit, accompanied by John Hudson and the other loafers, who kept with the hunters.

Hudson was armed with a conch shell, and he continued to toot it during all the pursuits. [To warn Ike.] The guide led Ike to one cabin in the black settlement and hid him in the loft. By some means, the pursuers arrived at the same cabin. When there, two of the [blacks] commenced a game of "fisticuffs," and were soon clinched and back on the ground, rolling down the hill surrounded by the other [blacks], hallooing and yelling, encouraging [one combatant or the other]. The excitement so interested the pursuers that they followed [the two] down the hill away from the house [and Ike].

Ike escaped from the loft and ran out the back door. A guide stood ready and took him to a vacant cabin in a dense wood, two miles away, the property of Abraham Pettijohn, who cared for him until the excitement had ceased. Then [Pettijohn] sent him on his way rejoicing. I asked John S. Hudson if he was not afraid to follow the hunters, blowing his conch shell. He said "No, the knots on the shell would hurt a fellow's head very bad."

Another who came here without assistance was a small negro, blind of one eye, which he claimed his master [had] knocked out. He said he [had] come from South Carolina [and] had been near a year on the way. He said that he had spent the winter in a cave in the mountains living on pork which he obtained by running the hogs down and then smothering them, afraid to stick them lest someone should find the blood. He lived here several weeks with R.I. Huggins, but would tell no person the locality he came from in [South Carolina]. From some obscure remarks he dropped, it was supposed that he had killed his master before he started.

Two men without assistance passed through this neighborhood, only making a short call on a colored family in an obscure location and passed on without a guide. They were followed in a day or two by their master on the hunt of them. In discovering them, he said "one of them was a young mulatto, with sense enough for a congressman, and religion enough for a whole church."

He stopped at a grog shop and tavern, started here for the accommodation of slave hunters. The proprietor made him believe his men were hid in this vicinity and succeeded in keeping him hunting here for a week or ten days. We never tried to disabuse him, for we proffered he should hunt where they were not, rather than where they were.

Two young men were conveyed here and placed in care of Esquire Kincaid, who hid and fed them in his cornfield until they could be forwarded on. Last summer [1892], one of these fugitives, whose name is Rankin, was traveling through this state soliciting funds for the benefit of a Freedman's College near Memphis, Tenn., with which he is connected. He [stopped] here to thank us for helping him to Canada just fifty years before. But myself and the boy, a son of Mr. Kincaid, who carried his dinner to the field (and who is now a gray-haired man), were all that are living who assisted him. He told of what the dinner consisted that he ate fifty years ago. But we did not know then that we were assisting a College Professor to liberty.

When [Kentucky U.S. Senator] Henry Clay was a candidate for President in 1844, a young mulatto man, a slave of Clay's, was taken through Adams County on a line east of this and whose back was still very sore from a brutal flogging he had incurred.

Another incident which did not occur on our line but I suppose is true: A slave in West Virginia celebrated for his Herculean powers started for Canada. His great strength made the slave hunters timid about following him. One egotistical braggadocio declared he was not afraid of any "[negro]" [and] he could bring him back. He started, followed him into the eastern part of Ohio, overtook him in a long piece of woods, ordered the slave to halt. [The slave] meekly obeyed. The pursuer dismounted, drew out his rope, approached the negro, ordered him to cross his wrists. The slave meekly obeyed again. As he was about to tie him, the slave seized him, tied his hands together and bucked him, as the soldiers call it, laid him by the side of the road, mounted his horse and proceeded on his way to Canada. In due time he sent a letter to his master informing him that he had safely arrived in Canada.

Still another [story] of different character. A young woman of Campbell County, Kentucky, at her parents' death, inherited one slave which was her principal fortune. This slave was married to a woman belonging to another owner who determined to sell her down the river.

On learning this, her husband besought his young mistress to buy his wife, but she told him that it was impossible as she had not the means. He was very much dejected and sorrowful over the prospects. After considering the matter, his young mistress advised him to steal his wife and flee with her to Canada. He followed her advice, crossed the river at Moscow, Ohio, arrived at Hoover's in Williamsburg [west of Sardinia], who forwarded them on his other line. Here was one slave holder who had both a conscience and a heart.

Setting the Stage: The Newspapers
CHAPTER FOUR

Prior to 1838, few Americans outside of Ohio and the abolitionist community had heard of Rev. John B. Mahan of Sardinia, Ohio. The country was about to be inundated with news about Mahan, his trial and his plight because of his allegedly breaking the 1830 Kentucky Slave Stealing Statute.

Not surprisingly, nearly all Southern newspaper editors, writing from states where slavery had been legal since the nation's founding, were vehement anti-abolitionists who viewed Mahan with disdain and fear. Most of their readers probably hoped, even prayed, he would lose his case. An example had to be made of him.

Northern newspaper editors weren't united in their opinions, with many Democrat editors writing opinion pieces that sounded more "Southern" in tone. Although generally realizing slavery one day must end, some Northern editors hated abolition while favoring instead the relocating of free blacks to Africa (Colonization), a popular sentiment of the day. Other editors feared enslaved blacks, if freed, could take the jobs of whites, or would be unable to support themselves if freed.

Many Northern editors were pro-abolition, with some in Ohio quite adamant, usually linking their views to the Christian faith. Sometimes these newspaper editors would have locals in a specific area attend abolitionist-related events to send first-hand information, in part to counter the expected anti-abolitionist editors who often did the same to employ their own slant. Pro-abolitionist newspaper editors often reprinted articles from other pro-abolitionist newspapers, especially *The Liberator* of Boston, Massachusetts, not unlike many news websites do today, i.e., linking to other news sources.

An example of how editors treated abolitionists comes from two stories reprinted back-to-back in the *State Journal* (Montpelier, Vermont).

The Ohio Anti-Slavery Society had just finished its second annual meeting in April 1836 in Granville, Ohio, just months before the 1836 Cincinnati Riots. The first editorial below reported on James G. Birney headlining an event in Xenia, Ohio, immediately after the Society convention. It was first published in the *Springfield (Ohio) Pioneer*. (Later, republished by the *State Journal*, of course.) The second editorial comes from James G. Birney himself reporting in *The Philanthropist* about the recent Society convention, also republished in the *State Journal*. You cannot find two more completely different ways of writing about abolitionists than that penned by these two newspaper editors.

FOAMING OUT THEIR OWN SHAME

An Egging: Mr. Birney, the high priest of Western abolitionism, addressed the citizens of our neighbor Xenia, last Friday evening, on the subject of slavery. The Free Press says, that during the delivery of the address, those outside the building would occasionally throw an egg into the door or through a window. The address ended, Mr. Birney and his friends were egged off the ground. But the worst of this egg work is now to be told. After the lecturer and his friends were safely housed, the eggocracy turned their artillery against the printing office of our worthy anti-masonic friend; and we are gravely assured, left only when the front of the building had assumed a beautiful straw color. We trust that this distinguished mark of attention, will in no wise render our neighbor Purdy (another editor) vain. He should bear his honors meekly.

The Philanthropist: We have just returned from attending the first anniversary of the Ohio State Anti-Slavery Society, held near the village of Granville, in Licking County. It was indeed a meeting of the friends of liberty and right, that cheered every heart among them. Although, for the purposes of peace, our friends—their meeting within the corporate limits of the village being objected to by many of the inhabitants—met in a neighboring barn, yet, we trust, it will be proved in its results, to have been a holy convocation.... The work indeed goes bravely on. Another year of persevering effort, and no doubt need be entertained of the State of Ohio—that it will be completely abolitionized. What matters it, that we have a village mob occasionally? That a rabble now and then of whiskey drinkers, and unmannered boys, assail us and disturb our meetings? Nothing. It hardly deserves notice, by the side of the great and animating success of the cause of freedom. It only serves to stir up the honest yeomanry of the country, for whose freedom, and that of their children and our own, we contend, as well as for the liberty of the poor slave. Liberty to the slave or slavery to the free is the alternative, and let it be the watch word.

It may be difficult for modern readers to fathom the importance the newspaper media played for people in that age. In 1838, for example, Internet or television didn't exist, the telegraph had not been invented (it still was six years off), and the telephone had not been invented. Nearly all

Americans received news and opinion through newspapers—or from talkative friends who read newspapers—and often the news sources were simply reprints of original articles in other newspapers.

The number of newspapers in 1838 was legion. Just Cincinnati alone, the economic and cultural center of Southwest Ohio, had the *Catholic Telegraph*, *Cincinnati Advertiser*, *Cincinnati Chronicle*, *Cincinnati Gazette*, and the *Cincinnati Enquirer*. Many people in Brown County and other area counties read Cincinnati newspapers. (Today, Cincinnati only has *The Cincinnati Enquirer*.)

Newspapers came and went. For example, in Cincinnati, again, some newspapers there lasted only months or several years, usually victims of competition. In the era in which Mahan was active on the Underground Railroad, in addition to the above newspapers, the *Cincinnati Chronicle and Literary Gazette* published in 1830-37, the *Daily Cincinnati Republican* in 1840-42, and the *Ohio Phoenix* in 1835-36.

The four legal trials of John B. Mahan may have occurred in Maysville, Kentucky, and Ohio, but public opinion regarding those trials was formed in the nation's newspapers. Politicians, similar to today, much preferred winning over public opinion first through various media before proposing or enacting new law.

It was no coincidence budding politicians owned newspapers to enhance their careers, such as Thomas L. Hamer owning a newspaper in Georgetown, Ohio. Another newspaperman turned politician was Warren G. Harding, who co-purchased *The Marion Star* in 1884 and editorialized his way into becoming a U.S. President. Similar to our day, readers knew which newspapers favored which party, and usually bought papers affirming their viewpoints. You could say societal and political battles were won and lost in newsprint, which became true for the public opinion battle over abolition, too.

Setting the Stage: Imprisonment
CHAPTER FIVE

In summer 1838, a group of frustrated Kentucky slave owners offered up to $2,500 in reward money for the assassination or capture of John B. Mahan and Dr. Isaac Beck, and of Rev. John Rankin and Dr. Alexander Campbell of Ripley. Too many enslaved blacks had slipped through the cracks; too much money and productivity had been lost. The homes and property of Sardinia abolitionists regularly were being searched by slave hunters, who sometimes threatened lives and livelihoods.

It was a dangerous world for abolitionists and soon became that for John B. Mahan. His world and that of his family would crumble and no one in the Ohio abolitionist community could have seen this coming—not even Mahan.

On August 8, 1838, Kentucky Governor James Clark sent a warrant to Ohio Governor Joseph Vance, demanding the arrest of John B. Mahan and his extradition to Kentucky. Here is the warrant, which was presented to Vance along with the indictments.

> To his Excellency the Governor of the State of Ohio,
> Whereas, it has been represented, by the affidavit of William Greathouse, that John B. Mahan stands charged by two indictments in the Mason Circuit Court of this State, in aiding and assisting certain slaves, the property of the paid William Greathouse, to make their escape from the possession of him, the said William Greathouse, out of and beyond the State of Kentucky.
> And whereas, information has been received at the

Executive Department of this State that the said John B. Mahan HAS FLED FROM JUSTICE, AND IS NOW GOING AT LARGE IN THE STATE OF OHIO; and it being important and highly necessary for the good of society that the perpetrators of such offences should be brought to justice: Now, therefore, I, James Clark, Governor of the Commonwealth of Kentucky, by virtue of the authority vested in me by the Constitution and laws of the United States, do, by these present, DEMAND THE SAID JOHN B. MAHAN, AS A FUGITIVE FROM THE JUSTICE OF THE LAWS OF THIS STATE, and make known to your excellency that I have appointed David Wood my agent to receive said fugitive, and bring him to this State, having jurisdiction of the said offence, that he may abide his trial for the crime with which he stands charged.

In compliance with the requisitions, I herewith annex and submit to your Excellency a copy of the indictments upon which this demand is founded, which I certify is authentic.

In testimony whereof, I have hereunto set my hand, and caused the seal of the Commonwealth of Kentucky to be affixed at Frankfort, the 8th day of August, in the year one thousand eight hundred and thirty-eight, in the forty seventh year of the Commonwealth. By the Governor. JAS. CLARK.

Upon receiving the warrant, Ohio Governor Vance on September 6 issued his own warrant—nearly a full month after Kentucky Governor Clark's request—saying, "under the requisition of the Governor of the Commonwealth of Kentucky, for the arrest and delivery to the authorities of that State of John B. Mahan, of Brown County, charged on two indictments found in the county of Mason, in that

Commonwealth, with the crime of 'aiding and assisting certain slaves, the property of the said William Greathouse, to make their escape from the possession of him, the said William Greathouse, out of and beyond the State of Kentucky.'"

On Monday September 17, 1838, Brown County sheriff's deputy Vince Crabb was sent to arrest and deliver Mahan to Kentucky authorities. Crabb seized Mahan at his Sardinia home, with his family watching and crying, and hugging, and Mahan wiping away the tears of his children. Crabb brought him bound to Georgetown, where attorney Thomas L. Hamer, Beck's former boss, absolutely refused to provide a writ of habeas corpus for Mahan. Hamer was "conscientiously" against abolition. Mahan and his captors went by boat over the Ohio River to Maysville. It had happened quickly. Mahan simply could not believe Hamer had refused him. Mahan prayed much of the way to Kentucky, not knowing at all what his fate would be. More than anything, he was confused about what was happening. It made no sense.

A writ of habeas corpus, filed by any Georgetown attorney, theoretically could have protected Mahan from being taken to Kentucky. Such a writ could have given him access to a Georgetown judge and the opportunity to press his case in theoretically friendlier Ohio. The government would have had to provide a sound reason for his being in custody. Technically, he could have proven that he had never been in Kentucky over the prior twenty years nor broken any of their laws and avoided the trial altogether.

Even later that day, when Mahan's friends finally did procure a writ of habeas corpus from a friendlier attorney, and had caught up to Mahan's party on the Ohio side of the river, Mahan's captors simply ignored the writ of habeas corpus. So, he ended up in heavy iron shackles. In a way, the September arrest and imprisonment came as no surprise once he learned Greathouse was involved.

On November 1, 1838, just before Mahan's trial began, Sardinia friends of Mahan released to *The Philanthropist* an account of the recent aggressiveness of Kentucky slave hunters in Brown County, including one involving Greathouse, an incident Mahan would have known about.

They wrote: "That for the last six months our neighborhood (Sardinia) has been unusually infested with negro-hunters who have in several instances and in various ways displayed the demoralizing influence of slavery. They have prowled about the neighborhood by night, watched the houses, and, it is believed, searched the barns and out houses and robbed the grainfields of our citizens."

For example, on June 25, 1838, about 11 p.m., William Greathouse and a band of twenty hunters, showed at the home of Lewis Pettijohn, forced their way in, threatened Pettijohn at pistol point, clubbed Pettijohn twice, stripped bed blankets off Mrs. Pettijohn looking for a fugitive, and threatened Lewis should he refuse to tell Greathouse the location of the fugitive.

In September, just a week after Mahan's arrest: "In one case a Kentuckian and a rabble of vile fellows which he had collected, about thirty in number, were prowling through the woods on the third Sabbath of last September (1838). As they came near a house, the occupant went out to see what was going on. When he approached near enough to see the company, judging their business from their appearance, he concluded to return again to his own house. As he turned, the Kentuckian saw him, and ordered him to stop; but thinking he had a right to do as he pleased, he gave no heed to the order. The Kentuckian started towards him and repeated the command to stop. The man then quickened his pace, and the Kentuckian spurred his horse to the gallop and overtook the individual by time he arrived at his own enclosure; and while he was in the act of jumping or falling over the fence, the negro hunter drew a pistol and fired at him. The ball glanced the rail where he sat the instant before."

With all this in mind and more, Mahan began penning in prison, best he could while in iron shackles, letters to the outside world. At least they allowed him use of his hands. Some of those letters would end up being published for a nationwide audience in *The Philanthropist* on October 23 and *The Liberator* on November 16, with the latter occurring literally while Mahan was on trial.

As reported by *The Philanthropist*, when Mahan was being taken from his Sardinia family, "...his children were weeping about him, [and] his wife, with a truly Christian spirit, took him by the hand and exhorted him to stand by the truth. 'Better,' said this noble woman, 'to die on the right side than live on the wrong.'"

On September 22, from his jail cell, Mahan wrote a message to his grieving wife.

> My Beloved Wife—this is the fifth day of my imprisonment, and the Lord is still with me in this my sixth trouble, and in the seventh I am willing to trust Him. Although destitute of many comforts which my own home furnished me, still my prison is a tolerable place. The prison keeper and family are kind and

humane—the Lord reward them. There are indeed strong stone walls and massy iron doors and grates, that deprive me of my liberty; but there is no unquenchable fire, no undying worm, no interminable hell, no indescribable anguish, no frowning Judge, no guilty fears, no haunting, midnight, frightful spectre, to chase my soul to mad despair.

I have water to cool my tongue, my bread is sure, and I am even richer than my Lord, for I have a place to lay my head. My peace flows like a river, my treasure is in the heavens; the bread of eternal life is mine.

Tell my friends and fellow Christians, I love them. I have received acts of kindness from them which have united me to them by a bond of union that time cannot sever. Tell my enemies I love and pity them, and would freely forgive them. My prayer for them is "Lord, forgive them, for they know not what they do." Lord, give them a better mind, convert them, turn them unto thee. Farewell.

Yours till death, J.B. Mahan.

On September 26, he wrote a friend.

My Dear Sir—I have recovered my health again to a goodly degree, by the mercies of Heaven. I am, by the grace of God, enabled to endure imprisonment much better than I expected. I brought with me a conscience void of offence touching all the matters for which I am indicted. In addition to which, I have the Word of God, the grace of God, the light of heaven, and the convictions of innocence. Not one painful heave of my bosom have I felt since I left home. Not one tear of bitterness or regret has fallen from my eyes. Not one moment's anguish, not one guilty fear, has disturbed my breast.

There can be no proof of the things alleged against me,

unless it is suborned. Excitement runs high; and my attorney informs me that there is something to be dreaded from that. But it is impossible for me to tell what the issue will be. Whether I am restored to my friends and fellow Christians or not; yet it is certain till death destroy my memory, I never can forget their love and friendship.

If I am not permitted to return to my family and friends, I have every confidence that every effort will be made by you, and all other friends, to keep my property together, sustain my family, and educate my children. I am in God's hands. Will not the Judge of all the earth do right? I believe it is only on account of the active part I have taken in the temperance reformation, and more, that I am here. And I feel now, by the strength of grace, that for the testimony of the truth, I could not only go to prison, but also to death. Whether God has any more work for me to do, I cannot tell; but if he will open a field, and show what is duty, that will I do. I endeavor night and morning to read and pray with my fellow prisoners. And believe me, sir, I have joy even here, incarcerated behind these bolts and bars. I am, sir, very sincerely your friend, John B. Mahan.

He wrote another friend on October 1, 1838.

My Dear Sir—I have been here in prison just two weeks, and shall have to continue here just six weeks longer until court; which will commence, I believe, on the 13th (2d Monday) of November, during which time I shall have an opportunity to ascertain whether I have any fund of Christian fortitude and resignation. I have been sick before and since I came here, but at present I feel much better. My health is as good as usual for this season of the year.

I hope, again, to enjoy the society of family and friends;

but if not permitted to enjoy such high enjoyments, I shall still have joy unspeakable and full of glory, and I shall have company too; for I have a promise, that God will not leave me, nor forsake me. I shall have the presence of the Comforter, for Christ, my Master, when he went away, promised he would send the Comforter; and I shall have the company of angels too, for it is written, "Are they not all ministering spirits?"

"Prisons would palaces prove, If Jesus would dwell with me there."

Yours, in the bands of Christian fellowship, John B. Mahan.

On October 2, he wrote again to his Sardinia wife, and to his children.

My Beloved Wife—Every day I look through the grates of my prison towards Ohio. I desire to be with you; but I am admonished by my Master, to be patient; God knows what is best for me, and often times, in my prison, amidst the clanking of chains, I feel happy, and am constrained to say, it is enough, Lord. I think I feel reconciled to whatever may be the issue of my case. My hope and my trust is in the Lord. Your loving husband JOHN B. MAHAN

My dear Children, I need not say I love you—you have had too many tokens of my love to doubt it. I need not say I feel the deepest interest in your happiness and an abiding solicitude for your everlasting salvation. I have spent years of toil and care and labor for your support and instruction and now I do ardently solicit you by the mercies of Heaven and the atoning blood of a crucified Redeemer, that you avail yourself of all the godly admonitions I have given you and all the efforts I have made to make you virtuous, respectable and happy. Don't forget your secret devotions. Don't forget your duties to God. Don't forget your moral responsibilities. Don't forget the honor and obedience that is due to your mother. Remember that during my absence, you owe her double honor. You will not forget me, and in your prayers I shall be remembered. Pay strict attention to your books; especially to your Bible. Do not be late at the Sabbath School, nor at the house of prayer and public worship.

My dear children, I want you to know that I am wholly innocent of all the things for which I stand indicted. Give yourselves no concern about that. I am in irons for no fault. I have neither sinned against God nor the laws of men. I hope to see you all soon and find you happy. Learn to be pleasant without being foolish. Learn to be serious without being melancholy. Learn to be firm, without being self-willed. Learn obedience without servility. Learn patience without stupidity. Learn to unlearn all your errors and finally cease to do evil, learn to do well. Your ever-loving Father, J.B. Mahan.

Polly soon visited her husband. The jailer gave them only a few precious minutes. To dress his leg wounds caused by heavy shackles rubbing against his skin, she ripped a portion of her undergarment and tried salving the pain with it. She asked the jailor and the sheriff to remove the shackles. But they would not.

Soon after, he penned these letters to a friend.

My Dear Sir—I have deferred writing to you until now, for reasons which I need not name. I am still afflicted with bodily infirmities, on the account of my close imprisonment. Perhaps you would like to know how my mind is disposed with regard to my peculiar moral and religious sentiments. I can say, sir, with a devoted apostle, "None of all these things moves me."

I find irons, huge beams of wood, massy stone walls, the deprivation of my liberty, and the scowls of unhallowed men, all sorry, inefficient arguments. They produce no conviction in my mind at all. It is no small thing indeed, to be severed from a beloved family, to whom I am endeared by ties indissoluble; to be carried out of my native State, torn from the society of thousands of friends, amongst and with whom I have spent years of happiness, for no crime, and loaded with *irons* like a felon.

But there is hope at the bottom of this bitter cup, that I shall become again a *locomotive* being. By the mercies of heaven, and the unceasing prayers of united thousands, I shall, I confidently hope, eat the bread of joy with my family and friends, immediately after court. [Next line unreadable.] "O, hope, thou blessed anchor of the soul."

But if my fairest hopes should all be blighted, if a gloomy prison is to be my lot, if I am to see no more the living, joy-bespangled countenances of wife and children dear; of Christian friends if I can taste no more the joys of social life, the sweets of liberty, heaven's boon to all, I am resigned. All my words, when added up, shall be, "Heaven's will be done." Yours, very sincerely, John B. Mahan.

By late September, Governor Vance probably realized he had been fooled after having been shown information from credible Mahan supporters regarding Mahan not having been in Kentucky over the prior twenty years. The *Cleveland Daily Herald and Gazette* published letters sent between Governors Vance and Clark in October. (See below.) Governor Vance sent the first note. The Mahan case now had become a full-blown incident between two border states a little more than one week before a major Ohio election.

His Excellency, Joseph Vance, Governor of Ohio.
EXECUTIVE OFFICE, Columbus, Ohio, October 1st 1838

To His Excellency, JAMES CLARK

Sir: Your demand of the 28th of August last for the arrest of John B. Mahan, and his delivery to your agent, to be taken to Kentucky upon the charge (in two indictments) of assisting slaves to escape from their masters, was received, and my duties under the Constitution and Laws of the United States, promptly complied with, by issuing a warrant to the Sheriff of Brown County; which warrant, said Sheriff executed by arresting Mahan, and delivering him to Mr. Wood, your agent, as appears by his returns, September 17, and Mahan is now, as I am informed, in Mason County jail.

Since this arrest and delivery, there has been put in my possession, evidence that cannot be doubted, going to show that there has been error in the case, and that said Mahan has not for many years, if ever, been in the State of Kentucky, and under our Constitution cannot be answerable to the penalties of her laws.

The union of these States, and the peace and harmony of society require, that the obligations to the Constitution and laws should be faithfully observed by its members, and whilst the chief Executive officer of this State, I trust I shall always be found to give force to these obligations by surrendering to the authorities of our sister States, those who may have violated the sanctity of their laws, and have taken refuge within our jurisdiction.

Yet I cannot consent that a citizen of this State shall be taken to another State and tried for an offence that he (as it appears by the evidence before me) did not commit within her jurisdiction, and who, if the evidence be true, has not been within her territorial limits. Under these circumstances, I have deputed Gen. William Doherty of this State, to lay the evidence in my possession, before your Excellency, with such explanations as may be required, feeling confident that you will give to the case that deliberate investigation that its importance demands, and that justice will be speedily awarded to this unfortunate individual. I am, with great respect, Your obedient servant, JOSEPH VANCE

Governor Clark answered exactly a week later and one day before the election.

Executive department Frankfort, Ky., Oct. 8th, 1838.
To His Excellency, Joseph Vance

Sir—Your communication in relation to the demand made by the Executive of Kentucky, upon the Executive of the State of Ohio, for the apprehension and delivery of a certain John B. Mahan, a fugitive from justice, is before me, together with the evidence which you have transmitted by Gen. Doherty.

When the proper papers, duly authenticated, are laid before the Executive of Kentucky, he has, under the provisions of the Constitution and the Laws of this State, no alternative but to issue his requisition; the proceedings are entirely judicial, and the Executive is only required to lend his aid in carrying out the faithful execution of the laws of the land; he cannot, therefore, arrest the proceedings under the indictment.

The position assumed by you in relation to the fact of Mahan having never been within the limits of Kentucky, is clearly correct, and if upon the legal investigation of the case it be found true, he will doubtless be acquitted. I feel great solicitude that this citizen of your State, who has been arrested and brought to Kentucky upon my requisition, shall receive ample and full justice, and that, if upon a legal investigation he be found innocent of the crime alleged against him he shall be released and set at liberty. I will, therefore, address a letter to the Judge and commonwealth Attorney of the Mason circuit, communicating to them the substance of your letter, and the evidence you have transmitted to me.

The anxiety manifested in your letter for the maintenance of the supremacy of the laws, and for the peaceful and harmonious intercourse of the States of Ohio and Kentucky, rest assured, sir, is fully appreciated and reciprocated by myself. With great respect, sir, I remain your Excel. Ob't. Servant, JAMES CLARK.

On October 4, just five days before Ohio's election of state legislators and a governor and just days after Vance had appealed to Clark, Mahan penned this letter to "His Excellency, Joseph Vance, Governor of Ohio," which *The Journal and Register* of Mason County, Kentucky, published.

Dear Sir—I have just seen in the semiweekly Journal of the 25th of September, a copy of a letter purporting to have been written at Georgetown on the 17 September, 1838, touching my arrest on your warrant.

Who is the author of said letter—I have not even the most distant idea, not having authorized any person to write anything touching my arrest and imprisonment.

It is no small matter to be severed from a beloved family and a large circle of friends, carried out of my own State, thrown into a foreign jail, and loaded with irons, having committed no infraction of the laws of my own State, nor or the State of Kentucky; especially when it is remembered that my very feeble health must be considerably impaired by two months imprisonment (the time of my arrest till the Court.)

But, Sir, I have not expressed any unfavorable opinion of your official acts in the case, nor am I now at all prepared (not having before me a copy of your warrant) to give an opinion.

I cannot impute to you any but an honorable motive; you could not have acted but in accordance with your convictions and an abiding sense of duty. But I beg leave to be regarded as not being responsible for any sentiments or opinions held or expressed by my friends, or any of my fellow citizens.

With regard to my arrest, it was made without tumult or unwarrantable violence. I was treated by Mr. Sheriff Wood, Mr. Marshall, A.A. Wadsworth, and others who came from Kentucky, with all that civility which is due from man to man.

Since I have been imprisoned here, several gentlemen have assured me that (though popular excitement runs high against any who are supposed to be guilty of the crimes for which I stand indicted) every effort should be made to give me a fair trial.

And now, sir, as touching the merits of the case, permit me, as a minister of the gospel of Christ, and as a man responsible to God for all my moral acts, to assure you that I am unequivocally and unqualifiedly innocent touching all the things charged against me in the two indictments; and further, that I have not been in this county, (Mason), neither by myself nor agent, on any business, civil or criminal, lawful or unlawful, for more than nineteen years, and that I have not, within that time, sent any writing or printed document to any person or persons within said county. Yours, very respectfully, John B. Mahan

For sure, the timing of Mahan's arrest could not have been worse for Gov. Vance and his Whig Party. A Brown County deputy arrested and extradited Mahan September 17, the state election would be October 9, and Mahan's trial was scheduled to begin mid-November. Vance did not have sufficient time to put out the fire, i.e., explain or defend himself to abolitionists before the election—and the Whig Party had many abolitionists. They needed every vote. Some Whigs turned out against the incumbent, and Vance lost by a mere 5,700 votes out of 210,000 cast. He had won in 1836 by almost the same amount. His party lost control of the state legislature and governor's office, even though Whigs nationally gained seats because of angst over the Financial Panic of 1837 and resulting depression.

In addition to the Mahan issue, Vance also had hurt his relationship with Ohio abolitionists by having failed to respond to any campaign questions regarding the possible repeal of the "black laws."

If Mason County slave owners in early 1838 had dreamed up a master plan that would force out Vance and replace him with an anti-abolitionist, bring in a more anti-abolitionist Ohio legislature, boot abolitionist U.S. Senator Thomas Morris (a Democrat, but not for long), bring in a new anti-abolitionist U.S. Senator, boot abolitionist Mahan, and cause Ohioans to think twice before again helping any fugitives, they could not have implemented this plan any better than what occurred in reality.

The timing of Mahan's arrest seemed fortuitous for U.S. Rep. Thomas L. Hamer, the same Georgetown Democrat who had refused Mahan a writ of habeas corpus September

17. Hamer had announced June 1838 he would be leaving Congress and not seeking reelection in October. Anti-abolitionist Hamer apparently had eyes for abolitionist Morris' U.S. senate seat, with Hamer literally announcing during Mahan's trial his intention to run for the seat. In that day, state legislators chose U.S. senators, and an anti-abolitionist Ohio Democrat state legislature might just elect him. Hamer seemed two-faced: By his refusal to file habeas corpus, he had opened the way for Mahan to be taken to Kentucky, while on the other hand, he was accusing Gov. Vance in a newspaper editorial of doing something similar.

The Western Citizen wrote: "We find in the *Columbus Journal and Register* the following letter from Mahan to Gov. Vance. It speaks for itself, and it speaks daggers to Thomas L. Hamer, the writer of the villain letter to the *Statesman*, which raised the hue and cry upon Mahan's case."

The *Daily Herald and Gazette* on October 30 could not have summed up the situation any better.

> Mahan was arrested and taken to Kentucky. The subject slept until just on the eve of election, when [U.S. Rep.] Thomas L. Hamer, [U.S.] Senator Morris, the *Columbus Statesman, Cincinnati Philanthropist,* and the journals of the party throughout the State, seized upon and distorted the facts of the case, and held up the conduct of Gov. Vance as that of a monster who had delivered up a citizen to the tender mercies of slavery and Lynch law, in defiance of law, duty, and the Constitution.
>
> Mr. Mahan was a respectable Minister of the Methodist Church, and a base attempt to enlist the feelings of that numerous and worthy portion of our population against Gov. Vance was made, and as we are informed with considerable success in some parts of the State. Mr.

Mahan was an Abolitionist, and that numerous and equally respectable body of our fellow citizens were furnished with a colored and exciting statement of the case by their organ, *The Philanthropist*. The effect was seen in the decreased vote for Governor Vance in the southern counties, according to our exchanges.

And later: The case was first bruited over the State so near the day of election, that but a small opportunity of informing the people of the whole facts, and of placing them before the public in their true light was offered. The Loco Focos made most of their well contrived windfall, and many our contemporaries attribute the defeat of Gov. Vance almost solely to the Mahan affair, with how much reason we are not entirely competent to judge. Now the election is over, and their end accomplished, the Loco Foco journals are dumb on the subject of Mahan's wrongs and injuries. The *insincerity* of their outcry is now apparent to everyone. [The Loco Focos were a faction within the Democratic Party.]

One person who knew Thomas L. Hamer well was Ulysses S. Grant of Georgetown. During the entirety of Mahan's arrest and trial, Grant was attending school in Ripley at the Rankin-founded Presbyterian Academy. He later would head off to West Point. Grant was but ten miles downstream from Maysville. He no doubt heard from local abolitionists much of what was going on.

Grant in his memoirs considered Thomas L. Hamer "one of the ablest men Ohio ever produced." Of course, his assessment didn't mean Grant always politically agreed with Hamer, only that Hamer was "able." Hamer and Grant's father were political opposites. Grant's father was a Whig.

As for Brown County itself, which was also home to Mahan, Grant said: "There was probably no time during the rebellion (Civil War) when, if the opportunity could have been afforded, it would not have voted for Jefferson Davis for President of the United States over Mr. Lincoln, or any other representative of his party; unless it was immediately after some of (Gen.) John Morgan's men, in his celebrated (Confederate) raid through Ohio, spent a few hours in the village."

Brown County abolitionists faced strident opposition from their own neighbors. Most Brown Countians opposed abolition, including Thomas L. Hamer. The battle between Hamer and Mahan was only just beginning.

The First Trial
CHAPTER SIX

On Monday November 12, after spending nearly two months in an uncomfortable and dark Kentucky jail, while wearing iron shackles, John B. Mahan felt hard-pressed on every side. He filled much of his time reading the Bible and praying. As seen in his letters, he tried spending some of his incarceration time rallying abolitionist support, keeping his family on an even keel, and preparing for his defense. He secured the services of attorney John Chambers for $300. Including Chambers, he had three good lawyers. He also wanted Ohio and national newspaper public opinion on his side.

He also painfully remembered what had transpired one year prior, on November 7, 1837, when abolitionist Elijah Lovejoy, who had been only a couple years younger than Mahan, became a martyr for abolitionism. Mahan said a prayer for Lovejoy's family. Lovejoy had been murdered in cold blood by a vicious mob of Illinois anti-abolitionists while trying to guard his printing press. The memories of Lovejoy, and the grave injustice of what had befallen him, simply moved Mahan to fight all the more.

Mulling over his upcoming trial, Mahan couldn't stop thinking how many of the good men helping him to fight had been born Southerners. Mahan himself had been born in Flemingsburg, only seventeen miles south of Maysville. Presbyterian pastor and Rankin associate James Gilliland had been from South Carolina, and Rankin, who raised money to pay for Mahan's lawyers, grew up in East Tennessee. Attorney John Vaughan hailed from South Carolina. As born Southerners, Mahan and the talented people around him understood well the Slave Power, the Southern mindset, their legal arguments, money, and connections. That gave them all pause.

Judge Walker Reid began his charge to the jury. It was this same Reid who owned slaves and had lost more than a few himself over the Ohio River.

Mahan could not believe the situation. It was surreal, given he had not been in Kentucky twenty years, hadn't broken any Kentucky laws while there—and yet, having been raised in Kentucky, again, he understood the mindset behind the Slave Power well as anyone. (Thank God he had not gone to Maysville to help free Eliza Jane Johnson. Doing so would have ruined his argument he had not been in Kentucky for twenty years.) He knew *they* already had lied to muzzle and imprison him, and *they* would not hesitate going further, even if that included twisting the law.

While sitting awkwardly due to his heavy shackles and staring up in abject silence at overpowering Judge Walker Reid, the exact same Kentucky potentate who had presided over the fate of Eliza Jane Johnson, Mahan listened intently to Reid's charge to the grand jury, especially the public reading of the Kentucky Slave Stealing Statute of 1830. He prayed under his breath.

Then Reid began meandering from his script and speaking out loud his own thoughts and feelings about abolition, in what John discerned as an attempt to prejudice the jury. The attempt certainly was in the least a thumb in Mahan's eye.

Reid appeared to be speaking to an audience far beyond the irate locals in this cramped, fifty-by-twenty courthouse.

Perhaps Reid wanted his state and laws to seem fair to Ohio and the rest of America, knowing a nation now was tracking his every word. Or maybe he was trying to protect his own reputation should the verdict not go the way his Maysville neighbors desired.

> Gentlemen of the Grand Jury: There is one other law to which I am impelled, by inclination, not less than duty, to call your attention. It is a law which was posted by our Legislature, long before the exciting fearful question of *abolition* agitated our hitherto peaceful land; long before the emancipation of our slaves was sought to be effected by means as unconstitutional, as they are dangerous to the safety of the owner and destructive to the happiness of the slave; a law which originated in a proper and jealous solicitude, upon the part of your representatives, for the security of your rights and interests in what now constitutes a large portion of the productive wealth of our state.
> This law declares, "that if any person shall be guilty of seducing or enticing any slave, to leave his lawful owner or possessor, and to escape to parts without the limits of the state, or a foreign country; or shall make, or furnish, or aid, or assist in making or furnishing, a forged pass, of freedom, or any other forged paper, purporting to be a deed of emancipation or will, or other instrument liberating or purporting to liberate, any slave, or shall in any manner aid or assist such slave in making his escape from such owner or possessor to another state or foreign country, any person so offending shall, on conviction, be sentenced to confinement in the jail and penitentiary of this commonwealth a period not less than two or more than twenty years; and if any person shall be guilty of enticing any slave to abscond from the service of his or

her owner, or possessor as aforesaid, or shall conceal any such runaway or absconding slave, knowing it to be such, within this state, every person so offending, in addition to compensation to such owner or possessor, shall be liable to an indictment, or presentment of a grand jury, and on conviction, be liable to pay a fine of not less than fifty nor more than six hundred dollars."

In charging you, gentlemen, as to the existence of this law, and inviting your attention to its penalties, I shall be pardoned for denying that the condition of our slaves is such as to require the kind offices of the modern abolitionists.—Have we, 'muzzled the Ox that treadeth out the corn?'

Our slaves are better fed and clothed, than many of our white neighbors whose sympathies are enlisted in their favour. If the interest and duty of the master does not induce him to treat his slave humanely, the Legislature has ordered the Judge of the circuit court to direct such slave to be sold and the proceeds paid to the owner. Formerly, slaves were tried without the intervention of a grand or petit jury; but *now*, such is the humanity of our laws, as it regards all trials, involving their lives, that they are placed upon a perfect equality with their masters, and it is made the duty of the Judges, when a slave is arraigned, if the masters neglected to employ counsel in his defence, to assign it for him, whose compensation is fixed by law; the right of peremptory challenge, and all those incidents connected with the more important right of trial by jury, are extended to slaves. They are capitally punished but for few offences, while for the commission for all others, stripes are inflicted, and for many of which the owner would be sent to the penitentiary for years. A proof that our Legislature has acted upon the principle that, where "much is given, much is required.'

I cannot believe that any country, however enlightened

by Christianity or philosophy, has done more to ameliorate the condition of its slaves than Kentucky. They are indeed happy, and if let alone would still remain so. Where "Ignorance is bliss, 'twere folly to be wise." The efforts of their pretended friends to educate them and emancipate them, among us in the present state of our laws and of public opinion, render their condition worse—they are riveting the fetters which they feign believe are irksome and galling still stronger, and *freedom*, like the cup of Tantalus, though presented to the lip, is still withheld, and still further removed from fruition.

The relation of master and slave is so wrought up in our social and political existence, that it ought not to be tampered with by any and every political or religious empiric; the consequences of its sudden disruption, are alarming to the *real friends of freedom*, to the philanthropist in every clime. It is a sacred relationship; it existed among the Jews and Gentiles, long before the coming of the Messiah, yet it is among his professed disciples that we find many of those whose sympathies seem enlisted in favor of educating and emancipating slaves.

I am mistaken, if they are not pursuing a course contrary to that marked out by their Saviour, or his great Apostle to the Gentiles, all that *twattle* on the subject of equality, to the contrary notwithstanding.

"Would any of you," said Jesus Christ, "who has a servant ploughing or feeding cattle, say to him on his return from the field, come, immediately, and place yourself at the table; and not rather make ready my supper; gird yourself and serve me, until I have eat and drink; and afterwards, you may eat and drink?"—Luke 27.

We are answered by those who are so zealous in the cause, it was a servant and not a slave—was it, I ask a servant that the Apostle Paul found belonging to Philemon—or a slave? I have been taught to believe it was Philemon's slave, and to show us by example what we ought to do: —the Apostle taught him Christianity and sent him home to his master.

   Rest assured that those who think they are doing God service, by meddling with the slave question, and making it a test, are as mad in their career as was Saint Paul himself before he was better taught.

As Judge Reid verbally assaulted everything Mahan held dear regarding the Christian faith and belief in black men as equals, Mahan had a righteous urge to rise up and shout in defiance. He held back. The room had an overabundance of Kentucky men bearing guns. He also sorely remembered what had transpired with Eliza Jane Johnson, even though Johnson later was released due to a request from Governor Vance and the kindness of Kentucky Governor Clark. He certainly did not want to get on anyone's bad side and have to pay the price.

He thought about his own personal experiences over the years. He had seen with his own eyes the mistreatment of slaves while growing up, in Ohio he had helped fugitives fleeing Kentucky and heard firsthand their chilling stories, and he had befriended former slaves at the Gist Settlement who had been mistreated by the Gist will executors and other advantage takers.

For whatever reason, at this moment, he could not get a visual picture of friend John Hudson out of his mind, and how Mahan wished he had ten thousand like him. They could get him out of this courtroom *and* end slavery in a month, he mused.

Unexpectedly, a wisp of hope regarding his own maltreatment and fate began bubbling forth from inside his soul, like waters from the deep. He sensed the Holy Spirit.

Judge Reid explained to the twelve-man jury how this specific Kentucky law should apply to Mahan, if at all. Reid was staking his claim as an anti-abolitionist, and making apparent his pedigree to the jury and slave-owning populace. At the same time, he was explaining the obvious limitations of enforcing Kentucky laws on Ohioans, to whom Kentucky laws logically could not be applied. Reid said:

> I repeat that your duties in the presentation of crime, extend only to the county of Mason. You must state the place where the crime was committed, to enable the accused to make defence understandingly; it is essential, and without designation of the place where the crime was committed, the indictment would be bad at common law, much more under our constitution, which secures the accused a right of trial in the county where he is charged to have committed the offence, and by a jury of the vicinage. Do not, therefore, suffer yourselves, by an honest enthusiasm for the public safety, or because of the alarming magnitude of the offence, to be deluded into a belief that this court can take jurisdiction of any crime committed out of the State.

The judge noted several examples of crimes allegedly committed outside a court's jurisdiction, including those of Erick Bollman and Samuel Swartwout, involved in the Burr plot and initially charged with treason on the "high seas," outside U.S. jurisdiction; and that of former Vice President Aaron Burr himself, initially tried in Virginia for an Ohio crime. He also offered hypothetical examples of how people could not be convicted of crimes committed outside of a court's jurisdiction.

Reid's final charge to the jury gave Mahan much-needed

encouragement, with Reid saying, "I have given you the law gentlemen, and no matter how slavery may be deprecated or defended, obedience to the laws is among the cardinal virtues, especially in a government like ours, where the singular spectacle is exhibited, of the governed being also the governors. Here each citizen participates in the legislation of the country, and is bound to support the yoke which he himself has been instrumental in placing on his own neck. Here a violation of the rights of the humblest man in the land, though only here on a visit from a sister state, is justly considered an injury to the whole, and the safety of the whole cannot be better consulted than by a strict and rigid protection of the rights of each. Whenever people forget, or disregard the law, and wrest from the constituted authorities their administration and condemn even the unworthy and guilty without the ceremonies and forms of law, liberty is in danger."

The Mahan trial was sensational news, reverberating in the hearts of abolitionists as a cannon ball shot into a fort packed with anti-abolitionists. *The Liberator* broke the story for a nationwide audience October 12, one month before trial. Ohio and Kentucky newspapers had been bantering since September. Now every newspaper in the country seemed focused on the plight of John Bennington Mahan of Sardinia, Ohio. Governors were writing back and forth.

Thousands of abolitionists and supporters across America suddenly were reading and discussing with their neighbors Mahan and his plight, with nearly all of them never having heard of Mahan before. Oh, but they could identify with him. If *Reverend* Mahan could be arbitrarily dragged out of Ohio to face Kentucky charges related to

Kentucky's fugitive slave law, when he hadn't been in Kentucky nor committed a crime there, then anyone anywhere, even Vermont or Canada, could suffer a similar fate.

Here was *The Liberator* review (and republication) of Mahan's arrest, including reports from a "well-known" Ripley clergyman, who was probably Rev. Rankin, and a Sardinian named "Mr. Huggins," perhaps the same Sardinian viciously whipped while returning from the Eliza Jane Johnson incident. The "Dr. Bailey" mentioned below referred to Gamaliel Bailey, then editor of *The Philanthropist*.

> A circumstance has quite recently occurred in this State (Ohio), which is well calculated to make every man unwilling to bow the knee to Slavery tremble from his liberty. On Monday, the 17th of September, John B. Mahan, a respectable citizen of Sardinia, Brown County, a local minister in the Methodist Episcopal Church, was arrested by an order of the Governor of this State [Ohio], and delivered over to the Executive of Kentucky, as a FUGITIVE FROM JUSTICE. The information (below) is contained in the following letter from a well-known clergyman in Ripley.
>
> Ripley, September 18, 1838.
>
> Dr. Bailey: Sir—I hasten to inform you, that on yesterday the Rev. Mr. Mahan of Sardinia, was arrested as a fugitive from justice in the State of Kentucky, by order of the governor of Ohio. He was hurried to Kentucky without allowing him to procure a writ of habeas corpus. Mr. Mahan is a local preacher of the Methodist E. Church, and one of the most upright and benevolent men in the State. The matter is highly mysterious. The demand

for him must have been founded on perjury. Mr. Mahan had not been in Kentucky for nineteen years. Imposition has been practiced upon our Governor. In times like these, orders of that kind ought to be issued with great caution. There was not the shadow of foundation for the demand, unless it be downright perjury.

So it is, this innocent man has been dragged from his family, a prisoner to Kentucky, to answer the demands of Slavery. This is more alarming than even the case of Eliza Jane Johnson. It has occasioned no little excitement among the citizens of Brown County. They begin to feel that no one is safe any farther than he may have physical force to defend himself. What shall the end be?

Yours, Veritas.

PS. Since writing the above, I have learned that a Grand Jury of Kentucky filed an alarming bill of indictment against him as John Mahan, late of Mason County, Kentucky!! What palpable perjury and imposition upon the Governors of the two States. What will not the protection of slavery lead men to do!!

Mr. Mahan is an Abolitionist, and his zeal as such has rendered him peculiarly obnoxious to slaveholders. Highly respected by the community in which he lived, even his enemies do not believe him guilty of the acts charged upon him. Mr. M says the Georgetown Examiner (a Whig paper), opposed to him in politics, and untinctured with abolitionism, (says Mahan) "is known here as a strenuous Abolitionist, yet, we presume, there are but few who believe the story of his having ventured to carry the war into Kentucky."

It will be perceived, that, according to our correspondent, a Kentucky Grand Juror designated him as John Mahan "LATE OF MASON COUNTY, KENTUCKY"; when the fact is well known to hundreds, probably thousands in Ohio, that he is an old resident in this State. We are informed by Senator Morris, that he has known him, as a citizen of Ohio, since the time he was a boy.

We have just conversed with two gentlemen from the neighborhood [in Sardinia] where the transaction took place. They say that the excitement produced by it is intense; the people are both alarmed and irritated. They tell us, that on the very days on which, in the indictments, Mr. Mahan is charged with having committed the acts referred to, he was at home, attending to his business—a fact to which several persons in Sardinia were willing to testify. [One testimony published below.]

CASE OF THE REV. JOHN B. MAHAN

A few evenings hence," said Mr. Huggins, "I called at the house of my esteemed friend and neighbor, the Rev. John B. Mahan—his wife seized my hand, and burst into a flood of tears. The children came around me, crying, Papa is gone!!! Papa is gone!!!

And what occasioned all this distress? The answer is short. Mr. Mahan was charged with feeding the hungry and clothing the naked as they fled from the land of oppression to Canada. In short, he was charged with doing just what the Bible requires of every Christian, and indeed, of every human being. This greatly incensed some of the slaveholders of Mason County, Kentucky, and by perjury they got a bill of indictment against him for kidnapping negroes from Kentucky, although he had not been in that state for nineteen years, and by this imposed on the Governors of Kentucky and Ohio, and made them believe that he was a fugitive, from justice.

He was demanded, and the Governor of Ohio, never suspecting a Grand Jury of being capable of such barefaced villainy, delivered him up. It is not even pretended that he was in Kentucky to commit the crimes alleged. And depositions have been taken; proving that he was at home at the times specified in the indictment. He was forced to Kentucky without the benefit of the writ of habeas corpus. Thus has a horrible imposition been practiced upon the Governor of Ohio, but which he has delivered up to ruin, one of the most upright and benevolent citizens of the State of Ohio.

What crime is too black for some slaveholders to commit, in order to protect their peculiar institutions? Mr. Mahan is now shut up in Washington (Maysville, Kentucky) jail. A number of the most-wealthy citizens of Ripley sent over a bond to indemnify, to any amount, any who would bail him out of prison, but no one can venture to go his bail.

Thus, by perjury and the blackest intrigue, the slaveholders have ruined one of the best families in Ohio. Mr. Mahan is a local preacher of the Methodist Episcopal Church, and lived at least eighteen miles from the river, and it is not even pretended by any, that he has been in Kentucky to offend against the laws of that State. In time to come, how shall the Governor of Ohio credit a Grand Jury of Kentucky? This is still worse than kidnapping Eliza Jane Johnson. It is kidnapping by perjury and intrigue.

This awful deed cries in thunder tones for the destruction of the bloody system of slavery. Let the sufferings and wrongs of this persecuted and innocent man inspire new zeal, and let the tears and cries of his helpless wife and children move every humane heart in the land, and let the horrid deed be spread before the world. Is it strange that perjury should follow in the train of robbing a many of liberty?

As Mahan sat in the chill of a dirt floor jail cell that

November night, wearing iron shackles, awaiting trial next day, much as he had the prior two months—winter was nearly on Kentucky—he began believing the Slave Power just might have the right situation in which to convict him. *They* could make a case. The trial was on *their* home turf, using a jury of *their* peers and employing *their* judge, the same judge that had dealt harshly with poor Eliza Jane Johnson. *Their* Maysville newspaper was covering the trial. Four of *their* lawyers were working for the prosecution—*four*.

If they win, God somehow will use this for his glory, he thought.

Obviously, Greathouse and/or another crooked individual had to have lied through their teeth about Mahan having resided of "late" in Mason County for the grand jury to indict him. The grand jury reinforced that lie by sending an extradition request to Kentucky Governor Clark, who forwarded it to Ohio Governor Vance. Yes, he had been born and had lived in Fleming County, Kentucky, but had not been there since at least 1820.

The next morning, with Mahan not yet allowed into the courtroom, lead Commonwealth attorney Payne asked for a short postponement in order to procure two additional prosecution witnesses from Sardinia.

Sardinia? Mahan had heard his hometown name mentioned through the courtroom door. *Witnesses from Sardinia?*

Mahan had three competent attorneys present: John Chambers, John Vaughan (a born Southerner), and Francis Chambers. The prosecution had four attorneys: Thomas Payne, Commonwealth of Kentucky lead attorney, and three assistants, John McClung, John Taylor, and Henry Waller.

John Chambers asked Judge Reid to allow Mahan to enter the courtroom. Once seated and composed, Mahan quietly but confidently pled "not guilty" to the indictment. Chambers therefore declared Mahan would be tried by a jury.

The prosecution evidence against Mahan began. They first filed an affidavit from William Greathouse, whose slave Mahan allegedly had aided and assisted.

The affidavit claimed Samuel Masters, a Sardinia resident, had been a witness to a conversation in Sardinia between Mahan and "John," a runaway slave of Greathouse. Mahan and John, according to the affidavit, "were conversing together, [and] it was expressly told to Mahan, by the boy John, that he was the slave of William Greathouse, who resided near Washington, in the state of Kentucky. Mahan in the same conversation, and at the same time, assured the boy John, that he vowed to fix matters for him, John, that he should not be caught; that none of them were ever taken after they reached his house."

According to Greathouse, Masters had promised to show up at court a day before trial, but had not. All Greathouse's legal team had was this naked affidavit. It was Masters, he said, who could prove the authenticity of a letter Mahan allegedly had written early August regarding John.

Mahan's heart skipped a beat.

Instinctively, and out of nowhere, he began humming a Charles Wesley hymn under his breath. His legal team could hear him, apparently, because their darting eyes were looking around as if they were hearing something but weren't sure what or where. No one else could hear.

> His kingdom cannot fail,
> He rules o'er earth and heav'n;
> The keys of death and hell
> Are to our Jesus giv'n:
> Lift up your heart,
> Lift up your voice!
> Rejoice, again I say, rejoice!

Mahan learned another Sardinia neighbor, named Hamilton, also had promised to testify for the prosecution. But Hamilton hadn't shown either. Prosecution attorney Payne asked for and was granted a two-hour postponement, hoping the witnesses would arrive. So far, it was not going well for the prosecution.

After the recess, the prosecution submitted as evidence a letter Mahan allegedly wrote to a woman he had believed was fugitive John's wife and to a man helping her, Perrigo. Secretly, Greathouse had employed both as a means to get fugitive John back and perhaps to entrap Mahan in the process. The letter dated August 4, 1838, read:

> DEAR SIR. You will take care of the oppressed for the Lord's sake. Send her to Mr. Johnson's, brother of the Rev. Hezekiah Johnson, ten miles north of Hillsboro, or to Thomas Hibbens, at Wilmington. The Lord bless you. Two o'clock in the morning, by moonshine in the street. Yours, JOHN B. MAHAN.

That ended trial day one. Led by an armed guard, Mahan trudged back in clanking shackles to his horrible jail cell, the chains making an awful racket. This was the place he had known as "home" the last two grueling months. The weather outside had been turning colder, with lows into the

40s. He did not know how he physically could take more cold should the weather worsen. Thankfully, the Kentuckians guarding him had treated him relatively well. He prayed the Lord's will be done and prayed blessings on them. He tried maintaining a positive attitude and yet couldn't stop thinking about the tragic fate of Eliza Jane Johnson and what this heartless slave owner Judge Reid had done to ruin her life. He thought, *if not for Governor Vance helping her....*

Pleasant thoughts at that moment came into his mind from above, when he most needed them. He thought good things about his family and friends in Ohio: Polly, the Gist Settlement, and John Hudson; Dr. Beck, the Pettijohns, Moores, Rankins, his dear children, brother William, the Presbyterian pastors in the Presbytery, and his fellow Sardinia Methodists.

He could not hold back his emotional pain forever, though. He had felt betrayed hearing two Sardinia neighbors had pledged to show up as witnesses against him. He had known the Hamilton family as Methodists from Slab Camp Creek. He never had done anything to hurt them, and had only tried showing God's love throughout the years. What had he done to hurt them?

Next morning, John heard good news. Lead prosecutor Payne announced to a packed courtroom that "all reasonable expectation of being able to obtain the attendance of Messrs. Masters and Hamilton of Ohio had vanished," and therefore the prosecution was ready to proceed without them.

John's shoulders rose and fell as he heaved a sigh of relief. He scratched his nose. One less thing to worry about, he thought, but he might one day have to see Masters and Hamilton again. All night long, he had been dreading the idea of having to hear Sardinia neighbors betray him on a witness stand. He had prayed forcefully and the Lord heard his plea. It had been difficult entertaining the idea—even the *possibility*—this could happen.

Who else would the Slave Power get (or pay) to bring to this witness stand?

The jury was sworn in, twelve solemn Kentucky men with distant, deadened eyes, who were not his Ohio peers at all, but from a completely different state and culture, who would decide his fate based on a Kentucky law he had not broken. He heard the jurors' names called, one by one, but did not know any of them. He tried making eye contact, but their eyes darted elsewhere, mostly down. Their names were David Henderson, James Brodrick, Samuel Carr, George W. Prater, Thomas Parry, Samuel Clark, Samuel Watson, Joseph Howe, Hensley Cliff, Spencer R. Howe, Thomas La Rue, and Reason Downing.

He couldn't help but laugh to himself, "I hope Reason shows some reason."

Mahan considered going against the stern advice of his lawyers and taking the witness stand in order to counter his lying accusers. People needed to hear his side of the story—the facts. But he had been talked out of it.

Once the jurors sat, Judge Reid read the indictment, word for word: "The Grand Jury (empaneled) and sworn for the body of the Mason circuit, at a court begun and held for the county of Mason, on the thirteenth day of August, in the year of our Lord one thousand eight hundred and thirty-eight, at the court house of Mason County, in the town of Washington. In the name and by the authority of the

Commonwealth, upon their oath present, that John B. Mahan, late of the county of Mason..."

At that, Mahan jerked his head towards Judge Reid to indicate he had heard the judge utter a misstatement. A few jury members looked his way. Everything seemed to be making sense. He thought, *late of the county of Mason?* Even though his attorneys had said this was in the indictment, he still could not believe it. The grand jury had acted on false information. A righteous indignation began burning inside his soul and he wanted to shout out loud again his innocence to everyone.

The Judge continued: ".... on the nineteenth day of June, in the year of our Lord eighteen hundred and thirty-eight, in the county of Mason, the aforesaid did aid and assist a certain slave named John, property of William Greathouse, then and there in the said county of Mason helped to make his escape from the possession of the said William Greathouse...."

John made eye contact with the three men on his legal team. He shifted weight from one foot to another. They all nodded as if to say they would take care of this. The Lord had been falsely accused and had kept silent at His trial, too, he thought.

The first prosecution witnesses were sworn in, their sweaty, shaking hands on a black leather Bible: William Greathouse and James Perrigo.

Greathouse took the stand first. He refused to look at Mahan. Greathouse said his slave John had fled his place in Kentucky on Tuesday June 19 and immediately Greathouse had gone in hot pursuit on a trail that would lead directly to Georgetown. On a Thursday, a Georgetown man told him

John could be found at Mahan's house in Sardinia.

Mahan mumbled under his breath, "Which Georgetown man? Hamer?"

Greathouse said he finished up unsuccessfully searching for his fugitive in Ohio, and returned to Kentucky.

Nearly two months then passed—*two months*—from when Greathouse had been in Sardinia in June, and his appearing again in Sardinia in August. Greathouse testified he had (*sneakily*, Mahan thought) overheard a conversation in Sardinia on August 14 between James Perrigo and Mahan regarding Greathouse's slave John, and saw Mahan give Perrigo the letter already submitted as evidence.

Perrigo, said Greathouse, accompanied that evening a negro woman claiming to be fugitive John's wife. But she wasn't John's wife. Mahan came outside with a rifle, Greathouse said, and ordered Perrigo and the woman to see John Hudson at the Gist Settlement. Perrigo refused. Greathouse said Mahan spoke loudly because Perrigo was deaf, which enabled Greathouse to hear everything clearly.

The rest of Greathouse's and Perrigo's testimonies are noted below. This and the sole letter were all the evidence the prosecution offered. As you will learn, *absolutely nothing* tied Mahan to being in Kentucky over the prior nineteen years or tied Mahan to breaking a Kentucky law while in Kentucky. (Read for yourself.) To win out, the prosecution would have to conjure up a *unique* interpretation of the 1830 Kentucky Slave Stealing Statute and sell that interpretation to the jury. *Oh, they would try*. But first the witnesses.

(In the style of the day, the prosecution and defense took turns asking questions of the witnesses.)

Mr. Payne (prosecution): Tell all from the beginning.
Greathouse: Mr. Mahan told Perrigo if he would go on to [John Hudson's], she (the woman) would find her husband. He gave money and a letter to Perrigo. Perrigo went on with the woman, and he followed them. He saw Mahan writing in the street.

Mr. Chambers (defense lawyer): Did Mahan write in the street?
Greathouse: Yes, he did by moonshine, at 2 o'clock at night.
Mr. Chambers: Did Mahan believe this woman was John's wife?
Greathouse: Yes, he did.
Mr. Chambers: How came he to that belief?
Greathouse: I don't know of my own knowledge.
Mr. Chambers: Did Perrigo tell him so?
Greathouse: Mahan asked if she was the wife of John, and Perrigo said yes.
Mr. Chambers: Was she really his wife?
Greathouse: No.
Mr. Chambers: Is she free, and what is her color?
Greathouse: She is free and about half blood.
Mr. Chambers: By whose procurement did she go?
Greathouse: By Perrigo.
Mr. Chambers: Did she go by your request?
Greathouse: I also requested her. She went with Perrigo, and I followed about one hour behind.
Mr. Chambers: Is she the wife of Mr. Woods Orange?
Greathouse: She is said to be.
Mr. Chambers: At whose instigation did Perrigo go?
Greathouse: It was first proposed by himself, after I heard from Ohio.
Mr. Chambers: Had you been before at Mahan's house?
Greathouse: I had.

Mr. Chambers: Did you tell him your name?
Greathouse: No, not that I recollect; I think he did not enquire. I told him I was from the Northern part of Ohio, buying cattle. Had he enquired my name, I would not have told him.
Mr. Chambers: Where were you when Perrigo last conversed with him?
Greathouse: I was concealed near them. Kile, of this county (Mason), and one of my black men held our horses.
Mr. Chambers: Did they hear the conversation?
Greathouse: No.

Mr. Payne (prosecution): Did you not conceal yourself when Mahan came out of the house with the rifle, to hear their conversation about your slaves?
Greathouse: Yes. I thought he would take the woman to John, and I would then ascertain where (John) was.

Mr. Chambers (defense) Do you say the woman is free?
Greathouse: Yes.
Mr. Chambers: Did you pay her for going?
Greathouse: Yes.
Mr. Chambers: Did anyone else pay her?
Greathouse: No.
Mr. Chambers: How long have you known Perrigo?
Greathouse: About 12 months.
Mr. Chambers: Is he a stranger in the neighborhood?
Greathouse: Yes, sir, he was.
Mr. Chambers: Is he your tenant?
Greathouse: Yes, for a short time until he gets possession of his land in an adjoining county.

Mr. Payne (prosecution): Did Perrigo go at your request to Mahan's?

Greathouse: Yes, Sir. When he heard they were at Mahan's, he said he thought he could get them by going.

Mr. Chambers (defense): Did he go voluntarily?
Greathouse: We consulted and advised together, and he offered his services.
Mr. Chambers: Did you pay him for going?
Greathouse: Only so far as to pay his expense. I had offered any man $400 to get my negroes, and he said he would not go for the money, but would go if his expenses were paid.

Perrigo was called to the stand, sworn in, and began telling his story. He had darting eyes. He said under oath that he had told Mahan in June that he was from the Ohio side of the river. A negro woman claiming to be the wife of a negro man named John had asked for his help. He asked Mahan if he had seen John. (At this initial meeting between the two, Perrigo was alone.)

Perrigo said Mahan had seen two negroes with that name, and one of them belonged to William Greathouse of Washington, Kentucky.

Perrigo said he asked Mahan if the negro woman could see her husband John, and he and Mahan agreed to a secret meeting the next Tuesday night at two o'clock.

Perrigo brought the woman to Mahan that Tuesday night, he said, and immediately asked Mahan to hand over John. Mahan said he didn't know where John was. Mahan insisted that Perrigo and the woman go to the next "friend." Perrigo requested a letter of introduction to the "friend," to whom Mahan wrote the letter submitted earlier in the trial as evidence, written in the street by moonlight. The questioning continued.

Mr. Payne (prosecution): Is this the same letter (handing it to the witness) that he gave you, and that you handed to William Greathouse.
Perrigo: Yes, sir. Mahan then asked me, if any more came to my house to send them to him. He said there was a colored man in Maysville who sent him all he could, and that he had helped along fifteen within a short time past.
Mr. Payne: Did he say that Greathouse's negro had been there?
Perrigo: I understood him so.
Mr. Payne: Did he say he would pay you for sending him negroes?
Perrigo: He did.
Mr. Payne: Did he pay you for bringing the woman?
Perrigo: He paid me three dollars.
Mr. Payne: Relate all the conversation that happened the first time you went to Mahan's.
Perrigo: I told Mahan a woman came to my house asking for her husband; she said his name was John, and he wanted to get some information of him, and Mahan said there had been two negroes at his house named John, and one of them belonged to William Greathouse near Washington, Kentucky, and if he would bring the woman to him that week he would help her to get to her husband.
Mr. Payne: Was it then he wished to employ you?
Perrigo: He said if it was any inducement, he would pay me if I would send him all that came to my house; that a colored man in Maysville, a barber, sent him all he could.

Mr. Chambers (defense): Was this during the first interview?
Perrigo: Yes, sir.

Mr. Payne (prosecution): Tell what he said about the connecting chain of friends from Kentucky, running all the way to Canada, of which he himself formed a part?

Mr. Chambers (defense): I object to the question as being calculated to incense the public's mind unnecessarily, without having an effect to throw light upon the indictment.

Mr. Payne (prosecution): This will open the question as to the whole fact, whether the prisoner can be convicted through agency.

Mr. Chambers (defense): The attorney for the Commonwealth had better withdraw the question and press at the conclusion, when the general question will be made. [Chambers said to the judge he was willing to open the debate and rest the whole upon this question, if the attorney for the Commonwealth pressed it, but he hoped he would not check the examination now.]

[The Court said he would be glad if the attorney for the Commonwealth would agree to the course Mr. Chambers proposed, but would not compel him.]

Mr. Payne said he could not surrender the witness; it would be too great a draw upon his liberality.

[The Court. If the Commonwealth persists, the defense has the right to open and conclude.]

[Mr. Chambers, upon consultation with the prisoner, yielded, and permitted the question to be asked; and gave notice that he would move the Court to exclude it at the proper time.]

Mahan became edgy. He glanced over at Vaughan and Chambers, who simply nodded once. His chains seemed to feel tighter around his ankles and he wanted free. It seemed odd, but he had felt at times over the last two months that this experience of having to wear shackles against his will had, in some ways, been good for him. It helped him feel what some slaves felt every day.

His three attorneys had prepared him for the very real possibility of the prosecution trying to convict him as an *agent*. It was the prosecution's only hope for conviction, they said. To put his soul at rest, they said no jury, in all fairness, could convict him on the 1830 Kentucky Slave Stealing Statute, even using the agent angle. *In all fairness*, he sighed.

> Mr. Payne (prosecution): What did Mr. Mahan say about the connection chain of which, he himself was a part, extending from Kentucky all the way to Canada?
> Perrigo: Mr. Mahan asked me if the negro had any money, and I told him not that I know of. Mahan then said there was a connection of friends who paid the passage of the negroes to Canada.
> Mr. Payne: How much were you paid for bringing the woman supposed by Mahan to be John's wife?
> Perrigo: Three dollars.
>
> Mr. Chambers (defense): When did you first go to Ohio?
> Perrigo: On Sunday previous to the date of the letter.
> Mr. Chambers: What did you say about your residence?
> Perrigo: I told him I lived on the Ohio side of the river. I told him that my name was Rock.
> Mr. Chambers: Is that your real name?
> Perrigo: Yes sir, James Rock Perrigo.
> Mr. Chambers: Who employed the woman to go with you, Mr. Rock?
> Perrigo: Mr. Greathouse, I expect. I had no hand in it particularly—had no hand in employing her.

Mr. Chambers: Under what name did she go?
Perrigo: Did not call her by any name when over there, but took her as the wife of John; that she was a runaway, and had come to my house; I told him that also on my first visit.
Mr. Chambers: What did you do with the three dollars?
Perrigo: I kept it.
Mr. Chambers: Did you consider you had a right to it?
Perrigo: I didn't know.
Mr. Chambers: Where did you leave Greathouse when you went to talk with Mahan?
Perrigo: I left him with the horses.
Mr. Chambers: Did you expect him to follow you?
Perrigo: I did.
Mr. Chambers: Were you a tenant of Greathouse?
Perrigo: Not then, but I am now.
Mr. Chambers: For how long?
Perrigo: For three years. We cultivate the farm on the shares. I get one half of all I raise.
Mr. Chambers: Where did you reside before coming to Kentucky?
Perrigo: In Pennsylvania, was raised in Washington county, New York.
Mr. Chambers: Did you ever live in Ohio?
Perrigo: Yes sir, in Columbiana County.
Mr. Chambers: What was your calling in Pennsylvania?
Perrigo: Farming and other business.
Mr. Chambers: Are you the same Mr. Perrigo who had race horses a few years ago in Newport?
Perrigo: Yes. I had one race horse in Newport.
Mr. Chambers: Were you ever in Mississippi?
Perrigo: No.
Mr. Chambers: Were you ever in Georgetown?
Perrigo: Yes sir.
Mr. Chambers: Were you ever in Lexington?

Perrigo: Yes sir.
Mr. Chambers: Where did you then live?
Perrigo: In Pennsylvania.

Mr. Payne (prosecution): Did you raise this race horse?
Perrigo: Yes sir,
Mr. Payne: Did you take pride in his blood?
Perrigo: I did so sir.
Mr. Payne: Did you think him a fine horse?
Perrigo: Yes sir, and I do yet.
Mr. Payne: Is there any arrangement to live with Mr. Greathouse longer than this winter?
Perrigo: No sir; but there is a verbal agreement to live there longer.

[At this point, a juror fainted. Perrigo left the courthouse and had a conversation with Greathouse.]

During the break, Mahan again felt he was being used as a pawn in a greater battle. He couldn't believe he was on trial because of this Perrigo, a *race horse owner*. It was God's will, though. Mahan's greatest strength, his compassion, had been his greatest weakness, and maybe would be his downfall should the trial not go well. His health could not tolerate much more prison. The trial had led to him being separated from his family and had caused great lament nationally among literally thousands of abolitionists. Anti-abolitionist Democrats were now in power in Ohio and he feared what they could do to him politically. Polly and the children were deeply upset, and they feared he could end up like Eliza Jane Johnson, a victim of the Slave Power. Perhaps God could turn this situation, Mahan's moment, into something meant for His glory?

Mr. Chambers (defense): Since you left the courthouse a moment since, have you had any conversation with any person about your contract with Greathouse?
Perrigo: Yes sir, with Mr. Greathouse.
Mr. Chambers: What is the contract between you and Greathouse?
Perrigo: A written agreement for the winter, and a verbal contract for three years.

[Mr. Greathouse was recalled as a witness.]
Mr. Payne (prosecution): Explain the circumstances of the contract.
Greathouse: There is a written agreement for the winter, and a longer time spoken of. We spoke of breeding cattle, and making cheese, but having bought another farm, I have concluded not to keep him any longer. He considers it an agreement: I do not.

[The sheriff supervising the jailor, David Bronnough, was sworn as a witness.]
Mr. Payne (prosecution): Is this letter the handwriting of Mahan.
Bronnough: It is my impression that it is.
Mr. Chambers (defense): Did you ever see him write?
Bronnough: No, I judge from comparison, having seen and read a good many letters written by Mahan, since he has been in jail, and which were handed me by the jailor to read.

[The jailor, John Hill, was sworn in.].
Mr. Payne (prosecution): Is this letter Mr. Mahan's handwriting (in the letter submitted as evidence), and have you seen Mahan write?
Hill: I could not swear positively, but it is my impression

that it is, having seen him write 20 or 30 letters since he has been in jail.
Mr. Payne: Would you swear positively to your own hand writing?
Hill: No sir, not always.
Mr. Chambers (defense): Did you read his letters?
Hill: Yes sir. I read all he received and wrote, in his presence, and at his request.
Mr. Chambers objected to the testimony of Mr. Bronnaugh and Payne withdrew it, as being immaterial.

The prosecution and defense verbally dueled over whether the letter could be read again to the jury. Chambers discerned the prosecution was trying to establish a link between abolitionist Kentuckians (such as the Maysville barber) helping fugitive John find Mahan, and Mahan helping John find other abolitionists in Ohio who ushered him to Canada—and together they would be links in the same chain and actively involved in the same crime. It was the only line of argument the prosecution had in being able to convict Mahan.

The judge allowed a second reading of the letter written by "moonshine."

Mahan heard the exchange. He coughed, clearing his lungs. He felt cautious. His defense team told the jury the totality of the prosecution's case rested on two points, i.e., whether Mahan had committed the alleged crime in Kentucky, and whether Kentucky had jurisdiction. Mahan didn't fully understand the legal subtleties of his being a link (an agent) in a chain of people assisting John and thus being convicted that way. His heart felt heavy.

At the end of this day, following questioning, Mahan's legal team strenuously pleaded with Judge Reid to dismiss the case because neither jurisdiction nor Mahan committing a crime in Kentucky had been proven.

An observer wrote about this part of the trial:

"The evidence on the part of the prosecution being closed, the counsel for the prisoner moved the court to exclude the whole of it from consideration of the jury as wholly insufficient, and incompetent to prove the offence charge in the indictment. Or that the court will instruct the jury that in the absence of any evidence to prove that the offence charged was committed by the prisoner being personally present in the county of Mason, at the time the offence was committed, he is not legally subject to conviction in this prosecution, and that the court further instruct the jury that this court and jury have no jurisdiction of this case if from the evidence they are satisfied the prisoner is a citizen of the state of Ohio, and had not been in the state of Kentucky until brought here by legal process to answer to this prosecution—unless he was personally present and aided the slave to escape from his master here or near enough to receive personal information, and give aid and assistance in case of alarm or danger."

Mahan held his breath, hoping his ordeal would end at this point and he could go home to Polly. Oh, how he longed to hold her. And reassure her. He sorely missed her companionship, love, cooking, and the happy smiles of dear children, including most recent, little Alexander.

John Vaughan read the indictment to the jury, word for word, highlighting main points. "That John B. Mahan was in the county of Mason on the 19th of June" he said, and, "That at that time and place he did aid and assist a certain slave named John, the property of one William Greathouse, to make his escape out of and beyond the State of

Kentucky."

Vaughan also revealed a number of holes in the testimonies of Greathouse and Perrigo, not the least of which was the fact Perrigo was deaf, which put his entire testimony into doubt. Then he said the biggest problem for the prosecution was in the jury having to believe "that a citizen of Ohio, living there, and never having set foot on the soil of Kentucky, is yet amenable to her law."

Vaughan started a well thought out and meaty law school lecture on the topic of jurisdiction, citing case after case, established law, Supreme Court precedents, the U.S. Constitution, and American history, all to shred prosecution arguments. He took no prisoners before sitting and blinking once Mahan's way, as if to say the trial was over.

Judge Reid opened the floor for the prosecution to have its say. Attorney Henry Waller started by making a case for Mahan being one link in a long chain, i.e., an agent.

> I understand these facts to be in evidence before the court: That the accused stated to Perrigo, the principal witness, that during the preceding month, fifteen slaves had passed through his hands, on their way from Kentucky to Canada, and of that number, two belonged to Mr. Greathouse (being the slaves named in the indictment)—that there was a line of posts, reaching from *the friends* in Kentucky to Canada, with the express view of forwarding fugitive slaves from this state—and that when they were once safely arrived at his house, they were secure from the danger of apprehension—accused at the same time, made the proposition to the witness to embark in the same enterprise, offering to pay him for his services, and when the witness hesitated, the accused assured him there was no danger, for that there was a

colored barber in Maysville, who sent him all he could.

Here sir, is proof of an attempt to hire an *agent in Ohio* for the purpose of aiding the escape of slaves. And as an argument to show that the service is not dangerous, the person applied to is referred to one who performs the same duty in Kentucky, without molestation. Is not the inference strong, that the barber in Kentucky; being in the same service, communicating with the accused, and pointed by him as an example, is employed by the same individual and by the same means, as he who is proved to have been thus tampered with. If Perrigo was offered a *hired agency* by the prisoner, are we not justified in concluding that the barber was engaged in a similar agency, anil by the same individual? And if the barber was a hired agent, shall we conclude that *the friends* alluded to by the prisoner, were so many agents of the same kind, disposed along the Kentucky shore? Certainly, the inferences are highly probable, if not powerful. I take the position then, as strongly supported by the same proof, that Mahan, the prisoner at the bar, by hired agents in Kentucky, aided and assisted the escape of the slaves named in the indictment; from their lawful owner. Is he guilty under the statute, and has he rendered himself subject to the jurisdiction of the state of Kentucky?

From where he was sitting, Mahan could see the facial expressions of every juror, who had seemed before this point to have no hope in convicting him. But what he saw he didn't like. Almost in unison, the jurors perked up ears and expressed a more positive countenance the longer Waller spoke. It was as if they had been searching for some legal means, *any* legal means, to get at Mahan and now they were getting it.

Prosecution lawyer Payne maintained the crime was

committed in Mason County, Kentucky, "by the abduction of a negro boy slave, John, the property of William Greathouse, and the crime was completed in the county of Mason, Kentucky. That the prisoner at the bar did commit the crime in Mason County, Kentucky, (and) by his *agents*, employed for that purpose, he, the prisoner, being at that time in Ohio. Those two propositions being sustained, I contend the venue is well laid in Mason County, and there the prisoner must answer to the charge; he being by the law constructively present."

Mahan anxiously tightened his toes, and coughed again out loud. He had been having trouble clearing his lungs all day.

When the prosecution sat, Chambers and the other lawyers on Mahan's defense team cut apart one by one all the prosecution arguments, again, as a skillful tailor would an old woman's dress. Mahan felt like pounding his fists and screaming his approval.

The heightened rhetoric on both sides had its moments, with prosecution and now defense both saying one verdict or the other could lead to all-out war between the states of Ohio and Kentucky.

He thought, *War between Kentucky and Ohio?*

Chambers cleaned up any doubts jury members might have had regarding jurisdiction, and reviewed the fraud perpetuated on the grand jury causing their claim of Mahan having been "late" of Mason County and committing a crime in Mason County.

Mahan was thrilled seeing the trial ending, win or lose. The Lord would help him through no matter what the verdict. Mahan instinctively realized, given his overall health, a conviction could mean his death in jail. It was time for

Judge Reid to give jury instructions, including his own legal opinion regarding what had just taken place. Mahan prayed again under his breath. Judge Reid opined his own closing argument to the jury:

> It is: that the prisoner has not violated the law of Kentucky, unless "he aided and assisted the slave in making his escape from the owner and possessor her», to another state or foreign country," personally.
>
> The crime must have been committed here, in Kentucky, to give this Court jurisdiction. It is so stated in the indictment, and must be proved as stated. No after act will do. No aid and assistance given out of this State will do, unless he was near enough, at the time the escape was effected, to receive information personally, and aid in case of alarm, by previous arrangement.
>
> But if near enough, at the time the escape was effected here, to aid in case of alarm or danger, by agreement, he might be said to aid and assist the slave to escape from his master in Kentucky, to another state.

The jury reluctantly withdrew to an adjoining room. After only a few minutes of review, the jury foreman opened the door to call Perrigo once again to clarify something Mahan thought was a minor point. After a few more minutes of silence, doors closed, the jury slowly opened doors again, but this time to announce a verdict. They shuffled to their seats. Not guilty. Mahan felt like jumping halfway to heaven, and held his legs out hoping someone would unshackle him right then. He nodded approvingly at jurors, who were all looking down at the ground in front of Mahan.

Many newspaper articles and opinions could have been chosen to summarize the trial, but this author believed the best may have been from the hometown *Maysville Eagle* on November 21, re-published in the *Daily Herald and Gazette*. You can just feel the slaveholding viewpoint oozing up through the newspaper ink.

MAHAN'S TRIAL

The trial of the Rev. John B. Mahan, for the abduction of the slaves of William Greathouse, Esq. commenced on Tuesday afternoon of last week in the Mason Circuit Court, and terminated on Monday. It appeared from the evidence that Mahan stated to the witness that, during the month preceding his indictment, fifteen slaves had passed through his hands on their way from Kentucky to Ohio or Canada—and that those fifteen, two of them (the same which are named in the indictment) belonged to Mr. Greathouse; That there was a chain, reaching from Kentucky to Canada, for the purpose of forwarding fugitive slaves.

Mahan further urged the witness to become one of the links of that chain, offering to pay him for his services. Upon the witness hesitating, Mahan told him that he need not fear, for that there was a colored barber in Maysville who sent him all he could.

The evidence on the part of the prosecution having closed, the counsel for the prisoner moved the court to exclude the whole of it from the consideration of the jury, as wholly insufficient and incompetent to prove the offence charged in the indictment: Or that the court would instruct the jury that, in the absence of all evidence to prove that the offence charged was committed by the prisoner being *personally present* in the county of Mason at the time the offence was committed, he is not legally subject to conviction in this prosecution. And that the court further instruct the jury, that this court and jury have not jurisdiction of the case, if from the evidence, they are satisfied the prisoner is a citizen of the state of Ohio, and had not been in Kentucky until brought here by legal process to answer to this prosecution.

On the part of the prosecution, it was contended that, by the statute of Kentucky of 1830, upon which the prisoner is charged, all who are guilty of the crime there defined, are guilty as *principals*—that the statute contemplates none as *accessories*. That the English law is expressed in assigning the jurisdiction over principles to the place where the crime was consummated, and whose laws were violated: That the crime charge in the indictment, was complete and consummated in Kentucky, and that her laws alone were violated: That the jurisdiction of Kentucky, consequently, attached; and the evidence fully supported the indictment. The motion on the part of the defence should, therefore, be overruled by the court.

Judge Reid delivered his opinion, in writing, on Monday morning, in which he decided, substantially, that the prisoner had not violated the criminal law of Kentucky, unless he aided, *personally*, in the escape of the fugitives from Kentucky, or was near enough to *assist* in case of alarm or danger. He permitted the case, however, to go to the jury, who had a right to judge of the law and the facts, with the charge that, if they found from the evidence the crime alleged was not committed in Mason County, they should find for the accused.

The Jury retired a few minutes, and returned into court with a verdict of "NOT GUILTY."

.... The arguments of counsel displayed a degree of legal research and close logical reasoning, rarely equaled, and we are sure, never surpassed at the Mason bar.

We are gratified, nay, we are proud to say, that the most perfect order and decorum prevailed throughout the trial, notwithstanding the courthouse was more or less crowded from the commencement to the termination. The position which we occupied, enabled us to overlook the assembled crowd, and if the countenances of men reflect, with any degree of fidelity, the emotions of the heart, there prevailed no excitement of feeling—no disposition to stretch the law to suit the particular case—but settled and anxious desire that the LAW, as intelligently understood and expounded, whether it acquit or condemn the accused, should be enforced.

Our fellow citizens of Ohio will perceive, from the result of this trial, that there is no disposition on our part to interfere with *their* rights or to encroach upon the sovereignty of their State. Have we not a right to ask, in return, that they will frown down the disposition manifested, by a portion of their citizens, to intermeddle with our rights, by inciting, aiding, and abetting the escape of our slaves, which we esteem *property*, and the possession of which is guaranteed to us by a common constitution?

On the same day as the article above broke, on November 21, a meeting of the Sardinia Anti-Slavery Society issued a report for publication, saying that for the prior year slave hunters and holders had shown an "unusual" amount of hatred toward Brown County abolitionists. The report noted rewards had been offered from $500 to $2,500 for the abduction or assassination of John B. Mahan, William Frazier, Amos Pettijohn, and Dr. Isaac Beck, of Sardinia, and John Rankin and Dr. Alexander Campbell, of Ripley, and William McCoy, of Russellville. At a later meeting, the Society "severely condemned" Thomas L. Hamer for refusing to file a habeas corpus for Mahan.

Mahan had faced six anxious days in a Kentucky

courtroom and in that time never shared his story with the world because of having chosen not to testify. He had been silent as a lamb. Written by Mahan, the letter below was included in a book about the trial and published 1840 for sale throughout the nation. You can tell by the way Mahan carefully constructed his words that he already was preparing for a civil trial with Greathouse. You also can tell he had been upset at the aforementioned *Maysville Eagle's* opinions regarding the trial.

> Sardinia, Brown County, Ohio, Nov. 29, 1838.
> Dear Brother Sunderland:—After an absence of nearly ten weeks from my "home and my country," I returned and joined the society of my family and friends on November 24.
> Perhaps it may afford you some gratification to learn the particulars connected with this very extraordinary transaction. Of the two slaves for the abduction of whom I was indicted in the Mason Circuit Court, one, (Nelson) I never saw, nor did I know there was such a human being in existence till I heard some time after that he had passed through Wilmington, a town forty miles north from my residence, and in the Canada direction. I have since ascertained that he was never within four miles of my residence. The other slave, (John), called at my tavern in Sardinia, on the morning of the 21st day of June last, and continued publicly (not secreted or concealed), in town through the day.
> He was at various stores and shops, and also at a temperance meeting in the evening (same day). He left for Canada without my aid, assistance, or guidance. Until he came, I had not known that there was such a man, or that William Greathouse was numbered amongst mortals. I had no agency of any possible sort in the escape of said

slaves, or any other slaves, at any time before or since, nor had I any correspondence with any manner of person or persons, orally, or by letter, or agent, or otherwise, for the purpose of employing any agent to abduct slaves from [Kentucky]; neither had I been in Mason County, nor any of the adjoining counties of [Kentucky] for nearly twenty years.

During that period, I had not sent any letter or newspaper of any description to any person or persons, transiently or permanently resident [Kentucky], or any other slave state; nor had I ever any agent in [Kentucky], on any business whatever.

Indeed, sir, there would have been as much propriety in indicting me for the escape of the Israelites out of Egypt, the burning of London, the gunpowder plot, the conspiracy of Burr, or any violation of the law ever committed, as for aiding and assisting the slaves of Greathouse to "escape out of and beyond theState of [Kentucky]; —and that indigested batch of stories detailed by James Rock Perrigo to the contrary notwithstanding.

Still I was indicted, and, in fraud of the constitution of our country and laws of the land, I was carried to a foreign jurisdiction, beyond the reach of my friends, imprisoned, fettered with irons, put on my trial, not before twelve of my peers in the vicinage of the supposed offense, but before twelve strangers in a strange country, men whom I knew not, of whom I had not heard, with whom I had never been associated, in whose vicinage I had never been; three additional lawyers being procured to assist the prosecuting attorney, hired by the people with money raised by donations and subscriptions—a thing unheard of by the oldest lawyers in the western country. And then, forsooth, because in the absence of all proof of guilt, I was acquitted and escaped with life and limbs, a certain Kentucky editor gives it out in broad terms, that the people of Ohio will perceive, that "there is no disposition on the part of Kentucky to interfere with their rights or encroach on the sovereignty of their State!" Indeed, sir, I cannot but regard this as adding insult to injury. It appears to me, that the people of Ohio can perceive no such thing.

It ought not to be concealed that Judge Reid, to his everlasting honor he it said, with all the coolness of a philosopher and prudence of a Christian, administered the law as "it is," and that the highest functionaries of [Kentucky], looked with burning indignation on the corruption, fraud and perjury, by which the most flagrant aggressions were made on the rights of a citizen of Ohio.

The trial lasted six days; the greater part of which was taken up in arguing the question of jurisdiction. During the whole course of the trial, no attempt was made, either by direct proof, or argument, or inference, to show that I had ever been in [Kentucky], at any time; but, on the contrary, it was admitted, on the part of the prosecution, that I never had been in [Kentucky]. Indeed, one of the counsels, on the part of the prosecution, did admit that I had not been at any time within five hundred miles of the extreme border of [Kentucky], and from this point he commenced a train of ingenious sophisms, to prove that I might be, (not that I was), guilty.

I ought not to omit stating, that I received acts of hospitality and kindness from Kentuckians which cannot be forgotten, notwithstanding the mass of the people, in a very extraordinary manner, encouraged the prosecution, by raising the hue and cry of "mad dog" by which my defense cost me ten times more than it otherwise might have done.

Who is responsible for this? Responsibility rests somewhere. How will the people dispose of their responsibility? Will they divide it among themselves? Will they charge it on the grand jury that indicted me, or the prosecuting attorney that advised the finding; or will they charge it on the individual, whose sin it was in "fraud of the law," to have me taken into the jurisdiction of his State, that he might with impunity commence a civil suit against me for damages, because his slaves used the legs which nature gave them?

Kentuckians have it in their power to do a noble deed by setting this matter right. Will they do it? Kentuckians have a right to investigate this whole affair, and settle the question of responsibility amongst themselves, as their court has the question of jurisdiction. It is proper, the people expect it, truth and justice require, that I should make an exhibition of the truth with regard to things attempted to be proved against me.

On the trial it was said by Mr. Rock, alias Perrigo, alias Rock Perrigo, that at my residence I told him there was a chain running across Ohio, by which slaves were forwarded to Canada. I never heard of such chain till it was spoken of on my trial. I am no link of such chain, and, although I am extensively acquainted with the sentiments and operations of abolitionists, I do not believe there is or ever was such chain in Ohio. This same witness also stated, that I told him a "colored barber in Maysville sent me all he could." But I did not tell him a "colored barber" *did* send me any or "could" send me any. That was the first time, according to my recollection, that I ever heard whether there was any such being as a Maysville barber.

I never was in Maysville till before my trial. I never held any correspondence with any person, either directly or indirectly in Maysville.

I never had any acquaintance with any person or persons resident in Maysville, till after my abduction, except the

Rev. John Collins and Richard Collins, Esq., and that acquaintance was formed in Ohio previous to their residence in Kentucky. This same James Rock Perrigo, under his oath on the trial stated, [said] I told him fifteen slaves had passed through my hands during the preceding month. Now, since the days of abolitionism, I am confident (so far as I have any means of knowing), not more than four fugitive slaves have passed through the place of my residence and in all I have never seen more than seven or eight persons whom I suspected to be runaways.

However much every good man desires slavery should have an end, and however much abolitionists are willing to hazard and sacrifice for this oppressed, degraded and despised portion of our fellow-men, I am confident that few, if any, for various reasons, would invade the jurisdiction of another state, to give aid or encouragement to slaves to escape from their owners.

But it ought not to be concealed, that a very great majority of northern people, as well those that are not as those that are abolitionists, (however much human nature has been marred by sin) are not capable of violating the sympathies of their nature or the dictates of their common humanity, so far as to be able to drive from their doors the unsheltered, unprotected stranger, or send away unfed, unclothed, unprovided for, the outcasts or wandering poor.

On the second day of my imprisonment, Mr. Greathouse commenced a suit against me at common law, for damages $1700, and in a few days he sent in terms of compromise, offering to send the witness, James Perrigo, out of the way (as he was not recognized), that he might not appear against me at court; and also, that I should be acquitted and delivered safely on my own side of the river, on condition that I would have deposited with his friend in Ohio, $1400, to be paid to him when I arrived safely at home. I declined such compromise, and afterwards he sent a proposition that he would take $1200! This, however, I refused, and consequently was put on my trial—The civil suit is still pending. Mr. Greathouse, after I was acquitted from the criminal prosecution, proposed by my friend, to take $800. The suit will be tried in May next.

   Thus, I have given you a brief sketch of the case from first to last, and you can make such disposition of it as you think proper. Yours, very sincerely, JOHN B. MAHAN.

A Divided Nation Reacts
CHAPTER SEVEN

Mahan and fellow Sardinia abolitionists celebrated their resounding win for a few days, if that, of what they would view in a couple weeks as a Pyrrhic victory. Americans in New York City, Detroit, Charleston, Raleigh, Boston, Baltimore, New Orleans, Washington D.C., Richmond, Cleveland, Cincinnati, Vicksburg, Pittsburgh, and more, all had read about Mahan. He was a local celebrity, of sorts. He told his Sardinia friends all he could about what happened at trial. They seemed to be looking at him in a different light, as if he had done an act brave beyond words. They were proud.

He had been grateful for all their prayers, he said.

The abolitionist landscape in Ohio and nationwide literally would change in a couple weeks as abolitionists began reaping the whirlwind of a stunning and unexpected backlash. Not everything happened because of Mahan, but his trial certainly played a role in shaping public opinion. As for now, though, Mahan could not see the backlash coming, and neither could his friends. Mahan still had Greathouse's civil suit to fight. William Dunlap of Ripley had struck a deal with Greathouse to get Mahan out of jail because of the civil suit.

Again, if Kentucky slave owners had concocted in early 1838 a master plan to eliminate, one-by-one, their worst enemies, no plan could have gone much smoother and been run more effectively than what was occurring in reality.

Lame duck Governor Joseph Vance tried suppressing abolitionist backlash. Before leaving office December 13, he issued a statewide thanksgiving declaration, which he had signed in his own handwriting on November 16—literally during the course of Mahan's trial.

He declared, "And whilst our invocations are made to our Heavenly Father, we should implore his protection and care in behalf of the poor and destitute, and that he would be pleased to put within our hearts the true spirit of Christian benevolence and charity, that we may administer to their wants with a liberal and bounteous hand; and that truth, temperance and piety may be cultivated and abound throughout every portion of our beloved country; and that he would, in great mercy, watch over, protect and defend the liberties of this people and the union of these States; that our laws may be supreme, our Government administered in good faith—and integrity, virtue, and gratitude, fill the hearts of our whole people."

In addition to this thanksgiving declaration, he apparently felt a deep need to justify to fellow Ohioans, and perhaps to Americans in general, his involvement in and personal actions leading up to Mahan's imprisonment and trial, which by this time he realized probably cost his Whigs abolitionist support.

On December 8, with five days left in his two-year gubernatorial term, Ohio newspapers published Vance's explanation regarding his Mahan case actions. It was one of his last public acts as Ohio governor. He needed to set the matter straight, apparently, in what many people today would perceive as an effort to rescue his political future.

> On the 6th of September I issued a warrant, under the requisition of the Governor of the Commonwealth of Kentucky, for the arrest and delivery to the authorities of

that State of John B. Mahan, of Brown County, charged on two indictments found in the county of Mason, in that Commonwealth, with the crime of "aiding and assisting certain slaves, the property of the said William Greathouse, to make their escape from the possession of him, the said William Greathouse, out of and beyond the State of Kentucky."

As this case has caused considerable political excitement, I feel that it is due to myself and the character of the State which has honored me with the station I now hold, that my views and opinions on this important subject should be made known to the people representatives, in order that they may take such steps in the premises as will best secure the peace and tranquility of our border population, and the rights of individuals in the adjoining States.

I hold that the Constitution of the United States is to be obeyed by all, as the supreme law of the land; and that it would be as unwarrantable an act in an "Executive officer," to refuse to deliver up a person charged with the crime of enticing a slave from the service of his master, upon the presentation of proper papers, under the demand of a Governor of a sister State, as it is to deny the right of petition, and the freedom of speech, and of the press, to the humblest individual in the United States.

All are constitutional rights, guaranteed by the same instrument, and of equal obligation. And as I am for sustaining that instrument as it is, I have not considered it my duty to set up my opinions of abstract right, in disregard of its solemn and positive injunctions. I consider the Constitution of the United States as the ark of our political safety, and whenever we reject its commands, all is put a hazard and uncertainty, and our whole population subjected to convulsions, anarchy and civil war.

We are also equally bound by a subsequent clause in the same instrument to deliver up those who held to service or labor by the laws of any State, and who shall escape into our territory, upon the claim of the party to who such service or labor may be due; and as it is desirable that the peace and harmony that have always existed between the people of Ohio and the people of our sister States of Virginia and Kentucky, by which we are bounded, and whose laws secure to them the services and labor above alluded to, should continue and be perpetuated; it becomes a high duty of the people of this State to adhere to the demands of the Constitution, and refrain from all interference with the domestic institutions of our neighbor States.

And when we reflect that this instrument was the result of concession and compromise by the fathers of the republic, to secure to their descendants the blessings of liberty, union, and repose, we cannot doubt the fidelity of the people of Ohio to all its obligations and demands....

In Washington D.C., a backlash against abolitionists began in earnest. Democrat U.S. Rep. Charles Atherton of New Hampshire, a states' rights advocate, within weeks of Mahan's trial, brought up five House resolutions for a full House vote.

His first resolution declared Congress did not have any jurisdiction over slavery; second, that citizen petitions to end District of Columbia slavery were a misguided effort to end slavery everywhere; third, similar to the second, tied the efforts to end District slavery to efforts trying to end it everywhere; fourth, that Congress "had no right" to discriminate between institutions of one state and others; and the first half of the fifth—that all federal attempts to end slavery violated the Constitution.

The second half of the fifth resolution read, incredibly to modern ears: "that every petition, memorial, resolution, proposition, or paper [presented to Congress], touching or relating in any way, or to any extent whatever, to Slavery, as aforesaid, or the abolition thereof, shall, on the presentation thereof, without any further action thereon, be laid upon the table, without being debated, printed, or referred."

In other words, in a free nation (supposedly, at least for non-slaves) that was founded on free speech, the U.S. House voted in favor on this date to prohibit free speech among its *own members*. Amazingly, this part of the fifth resolution passed 126-78. No other resolution garnered more than 65 nays.

Ohio U.S. Senator Thomas Morris went down fighting, though. He forcefully opposed anti-abolitionists like Senator Henry Clay on the Senate floor February 9, spoke freely about the existence of a "Slave Power," and said he was for emancipation and "against the great power of these two interests—the slave power of the South and banking power of the North, which are now united to rule this country." He called the Slave Power "this goliath of all monopolies."

You could have heard a pin drop on the Senate floor.

His oration cost him a Senate seat, and Mahan and Beck a friend and Capitol Hill ally. Even though Morris was a Democrat, there was no way a strongly anti-abolitionist Ohio state legislature in 1839 would re-elect a now ardent, open abolitionist. (State legislatures elected senators directly until 1913.) The new senator would be anti-abolitionist Democrat Benjamin Tappan, whose brother co-founded the American Anti-Slavery Society. Morris was out of a job March 4.

The General Assembly of Ohio, in January 1839, following the election, was dominated top-to-bottom by anti-abolitionist forces. The Legislature began right away an anti-abolition public relations campaign by passing its own resolutions: one said Congress had no jurisdiction over slavery in slaveholding states; another, that agitation regarding slavery in non-slaveholding states was "no good" and the conditions of slaves were not enhanced; and, all attempts to abolish slavery violated the U.S. Constitution.

Another resolution called for the sending of copies of the passed resolutions to the White House, Congress, and to every governor.

Two more Ohio General Assembly resolutions (mentioned below) caused Mahan to roll eyes at the Kentucky court system and Greathouse. But Mahan would not give in. He would only work harder against eradicating the sin and stain of slavery. And pray harder. The Slave Power was pushing back—harder than anyone ever imagined.

> Resolved, That in the opinion of this General Assembly, it is unwise, impolitic, and inexpedient, to repeal any law now in force, imposing disabilities upon black and mulatto persons, thus placing them upon an equality with the whites, so far as the Legislature can do, and indirectly inviting the black population of other States to emigrate to this State, to the manifest injury of the public interest.

> Resolved, That the schemes of the Abolitionists, for the pretended happiness of the slaves, are, in the opinion of this General Assembly, wild, delusive, and fanatical; and have a direct tendency to destroy the harmony of the Union, to rivet the chain of the slaves, and to destroy the

perpetuity of our free institutions.

Down in Kentucky, hilly land of fast race horses, beautiful bluegrass and slavery, a resolution proposed by the state senator from Maysville passed in the Kentucky Senate. It allowed for the appointment, of what today would be called lobbyists, to travel to Columbus, Ohio, and lobby the Ohio Legislature to adopt "some law to restrain its [Ohio's] citizens from interfering with the relations of master and slave in the State of Kentucky."

About this proposal, not yet passed by the Kentucky House, the *Daily Herald and Gazette* re-published a December 20 *Maysville Monitor* article, which tied the legislative proposal *directly* to Mahan.

> The developments in the case of Mahan, have shown conclusively, that the interference of the abolitionists of Ohio, with the slave of this State has carried to an alarming extent, and lest they should become emboldened by his acquittal, the State of Ohio owes it to Kentucky to adopt some speedy restrictive measures. We have no doubt her sense of justice, will prompt her to grant all that in reason our Legislature can ask.
>
> Would it not be well for the law givers of Kentucky to inquire into a recent outrage, under the form of law, perpetrated upon a citizen of Ohio. It is an object of some importance to the people of Ohio to be protected from such violation of their rights in future, and if we are to have any legislation upon the matter, we trust it will be designed for the security of our citizens from similar outrages.
>
> Meantime it would not ill-become the Legislature of Kentucky to define the duties of Grand Juries, to enact a law for the more effectual prevention of perjury; and to

indemnify Mr. John B. Mahan for his time and expenses during his detention in Kentucky.

As to Abolitionists being emboldened by Mahan's acquittal, is there no danger that perjurers will be emboldened by the non-prosecution of men who have been palpably guilty of that crime.

The *Columbus Statesman*, which shed so many crocodile tears over Mr. Mahan's case before the election, is in favor of yielding to this modest request from Kentucky.

The two well-heeled Kentucky lobbyists chosen at the state capitol in Frankfort to influence Ohio lawmakers into writing new law had pedigree. On January 26, 1839, Ohio Governor Wilson Shannon presented a letter to the Ohio General Assembly, stating, "Gentlemen: I herewith transmit to you a communication from the Hon. James T. Morehead [former Kentucky Governor], and the Hon. J. Speed Smith [former Kentucky Speaker of the House], Commissioners appointed by the State of Kentucky, under resolutions passed by the Legislature of that State, January 4th, 1839, a copy of which has been heretofore transmitted to your honorable body. Having but one copy of the communication, it is sent to the Senate."

Four days later, on January 30, the Ohio Senate reviewed communication sent to Governor Shannon by the Kentucky commissioners. Ohio Sen. Benjamin Wade, an avid abolitionist, offered the following resolution to counter.

> Resolved, That the standing committee on the judiciary be instructed to inquire as to the truth of the charges and allegations contained in the communication of the Hon. James T. Morehead and the Hon. J. Speed Smith, commissioners of the State of Kentucky, against the

people of this State; and especially whether the citizens of this State, or any of them, have been engaged in enticing slaves in the State of Kentucky to run away or leave their masters; and how, when, and by what means the same has been effected.

And that the said committee be, at the same time, instructed to inquire whether the rights of our own free white or colored people, or any of them, while residing within this State, and under the protection of the laws thereof, have been violated by the citizens of any other State, under color of such person or persons being fugitives from justice, or slaves from other States, or otherwise.

And whether the laws of this State now in force are sufficient for the security and protection of our own citizens in this respect. And that said committee report to this Senate, at as early a day as practicable, all the evidence in relation thereto, with their opinion thereon. And to this end said committee be empowered to send for persons and papers, and to examine witnesses on oath touching the same.

The Ohio Senate voted to postpone his measure, of course. The next day, January 31, an impatient Ohio House pushed the issue on the Ohio Senate by adopting its own resolution, "providing for printing certain copies of the special message of the Governor, transmitting the communication from Messrs. Morehead and Smith, commissioners from the legislature of Kentucky, to which the concurrence of the Senate is requested."

No doubt sensing a momentum change, Ohio Rep. Isaiah Morris, a Whig of Clinton County, just north of Brown County and home of many Quakers, offered a number of petitions from constituents, including ones asking for the repeal of a law restricting the "education of persons of color by depriving them of all participation in the school fund arising from donations made by Congress—and also for the repeal of the law prohibiting persons of color from testifying in courts of justice."

These petitions were ceremoniously assigned to various committees, where they met quick death.

He presented constituent petitions from Clinton Countians asking for repeal of all laws in the State "which make any distinction among the inhabitants on account of color."

Anti-abolitionist Democrats referred that petition to the judiciary committee, too.

Another Morris constituent petition asked for "legislative enactment for securing to all persons within the State of Ohio the right of trial by jury in all cases affecting personal liberty, and particularly in all cases where persons are claimed as fugitives from labor."

Of course, this petition would die.

Ohio abolitionists, just like U.S. Sen. Morris, went down fighting. Sen. Charles White of Brown County presented a petition from eighty-four Ripley women asking for repeal of Ohio laws making distinctions among inhabitants on account of color.

Sen. Benjamin Wade, of Northern Ohio, presented constituent petitions protesting admission of any slave-holding State into the union, the extension of the right of trial by jury, repeal of certain laws imposing disabilities upon persons of color, repeal of laws making any distinction among the inhabitants of this State on account of color—even a petition to protest the annexation of slave-holding

Texas. These were referred to the judiciary committee.

(An abolitionist since the 1830s, Ohio State Senator Benjamin Wade one day would become Ohio U.S. Senator Benjamin Wade, and in 1868 nearly *U.S. President Benjamin Wade*, when President Andrew Johnson somehow survived impeachment by one vote. Then, Wade was U.S. Senate president pro tempore and next in line to the presidency, since Andrew Johnson did not have a vice president his entire four years in office.)

By sending petitions to state and federal governments, even though often ignored, abolitionists pressed the issue and raised awareness. Former U.S. President and Massachusetts Congressman John Quincy Adams used the practice extensively, which worked well at raising awareness on the federal level until anti-abolitionist groups ended debate. Temperance advocates often used the same tactic.

The Western Citizen of Paris, Kentucky, reported on a special petition before the Ohio Legislature. "The Rev. John B. Mahan has petitioned the Legislature of Ohio for a redress of grievances, and renumeration for losses gained by his arrest and imprisonment in the jail of this county. His petition was referred to the judiciary committee of the Senate." It was Sen. Benjamin Wade who presented Mahan's relief petition. It died, too.

In an amendment fight February 19 to a proposed Senate bill regarding a fugitive slave act, Sen. Wade and other abolitionist senators made challenges, but their efforts had the same effect as throwing snowballs at a raging fire. They were outnumbered. Abolitionists had the support of only half the Whigs. A number of pro-abolitionist Ohio state senators desperately proposed a flurry of last-minute amendments, but to no avail. The 1839 Ohio Fugitive Slave

Act passed the Ohio Senate and House overwhelmingly.

As expected, *The Philanthropist* would have harsh words for the law, saying, "The Black Law of 1838-39, that bill of abominations, that thing, that monstrous thing that was conceived in sin and brought forth in iniquity, that converts the ministerial officers of Ohio into hunting dogs to go at the bidding of southern tyrants like bloodhounds, that howl on the trail of frightened fugitives, whose only sin is that they love liberty—that unhallowed enactment of mercenary legislature, that makes it penal to exercise benevolence towards a man with a colored skin, and that recognizes (contrary to our constitution) the rightful existence of slavery in the free state of Ohio."

Below contains the entire 1839 Ohio Fugitive Slave Law to help the reader understand its breadth, depth, and enormity. It could not have been any more restrictive towards abolitionists had Kentucky slave masters written the Law themselves—and indeed, they may have, through the efforts of Kentucky lobbyists. It was pervasive, it was invasive, and it was excessive. It was like taking a knife to Mahan's heart.

Sect. I. That when any person held to labor or service in *any* of the United States, under the laws thereof, shall escape into this state (Ohio), the person to whom such labor or service is due, his or her agent or attorney, is hereby authorized to apply to any judge of any court of record in this state, or to any justice of the peace, or to the mayor of any city or town corporate, who, on such application, shall issue his warrant, under his hand and seal, and directed to the sheriff or constable of any county in this state, authorizing and directing said sheriff or constable to seize and arrest the said fugitive, who shall be named in the said warrant; and in case the said fugitive shall be arrested in the county in which said warrant may be issued, to bring him or her before some judge of a court of record of this state residing within such county, or in case the said fugitive shall be arrested in any other county than the county in which the warrant may be issued, then to take him or her before some judge of a court of record in this state, residing in the county in which such arrest is made: provided, however, that no such warrant shall be returned before any officer residing out of the county in which the same may have been issued, unless the official character of the judge or justice, issuing the same, shall be duly authenticated by the seal and certificate of the clerk of the supreme court or court of common pleas; and if issued by a mayor of any city or town corporate, the official character of said mayor shall be duly authenticated under the seal of said city or town corporate; which said warrant shall be in the form and to the effect following, that is to say:

The State of Ohio, -------------- county, SS. To any sheriff or constable of the State of Ohio, greeting: This is to authorize and require you to seize and arrest the body of------------- sworn *(or* affirmed) to be the slave (or servant, *(as the case may be,)* of -------- of the state of ------------; and in case such arrest be made in this county, to bring such person so arrested forthwith before some judge of a court of record of this state residing within this county; or in case such arrest be made in any other county in this state, then to take said person so arrested before some judge of a court of record of this state, residing within the county in which such arrest may be made, to be dealt with as the law directs. To which warrant shall be annexed a copy of the oath or affirmation herein before specified; by virtue of which warrant the said fugitive named therein shall be arrested by the officer to whom it is directed, in any county of this state: provided, that no such arrest shall be made by any sheriff or constable of this state without the limits of his own proper county.

Sect. II. The said person so claimed as a fugitive, when so arrested, shall be brought before the officer as directed in the first section of this act; and the said claimant, his or her agent or attorney, having first given security for the costs, and having proved to the satisfaction of such officer, that the person so seized and arrested doth under the laws of the state from which he or she fled, owe service or labor to the person claiming him or her, it shall be the duty of such judge to give a certificate thereof to such claimant, his or her agent or attorney, which shall be sufficient authority for removing the said fugitive to the state from which he or she fled; but no such certificate shall be deemed a sufficient authority for the removal of such fugitive, under the provisions of this act, unless the official character of the officer giving his name, be duly authenticated according to the provisions of this act, in relation to the issuing of warrants.

Sect. III. If any person or persons shall knowingly and willfully prevent such sheriff or constable from arresting such fugitive from labor or service as aforesaid, or shall knowingly and willfully obstruct or hinder such sheriff or constable in making such arrest; or shall knowingly and willfully hinder or obstruct any claimant, his or her agent or attorney, having the certificate provided for in the second section of this act, in the removal of such fugitive to the state from which he or she fled; or shall rescue, or aid and abet in the rescue of such fugitive from such sheriff, constable, claimant, agent or attorney; or if two or more persons shall assemble together with intent to obstruct, hinder or interrupt such sheriff or constable in arresting such fugitive, or with intent to obstruct, hinder or interrupt such claimant, agent or attorney having the certificate afore said, in the removal of such fugitive to the state from which he or she fled, and shall make any movement or preparation therefore, every person so offending shall, upon conviction thereof, by indictment. be fined in any sum not exceeding five hundred dollars, or be imprisoned in the jail of the county not exceeding sixty days, at the discretion of the court; and shall moreover be liable in an action at the suit of the person claiming such labor or service.

Sect. IV. That when said fugitive shall be brought before the judge, agreeably to the provisions of this act, on the return of the warrant, if the claimant, his or her agent or attorney, shall not be prepared for trial, and shall make oath or affirmation that he or she does verily believe that the person so arrested is a fugitive from labor or service in another state, and that if allowed time, he or she will be able to produce satisfactory evidence that the person so arrested does owe such labor or service, it shall he the duty of such judge to postpone the trial to such time as he may deem reasonable, not exceeding sixty days; and in case of such postponement, it shall and may be lawful for said judge, (unless the person so arrested shall enter into bond, with one or more sufficient securities, to be approved of by such judge, in the penal sum of one thousand dollars to the person claiming the person so arrested as aforesaid, conditioned for his or her appearance on the day to which the trial shall be postponed, and that he or she will then and there abide the decision of the judge who shall try the case, to commit the party arrested to the jail of the county where the trial is pending, there to be detained at the expense of the claimant, his agent or attorney, until the day set for trial by said judge. And in case the party arrested shall be committed to the jail of the county, the claimant, his or her agent or attorney, shall pay down to said judge, for the use of the person entitled thereto, the amount of the jail fees and the sheriff's fees for keeping and providing for such person, during the period that he or she shall be imprisoned as aforesaid. And the said judge shall, in like manner, give time, not exceeding sixty days, for the production of evidence on behalf of the party arrested, if he or she shall file an affidavit that he or she does not owe labor or service to the claimant, and that affiant verily believes that he or she will be able to produce evidence to that effect: provided, that the person so arrested shall give bond and security as aforesaid, in the penalty of one thousand dollars, and conditioned for his or her personal appearance at the time and place of trial, and that he or she will abide the decision of the judge who shall try the case; and on failure to give such bond and security, the party arrested shall be committed to the jail of the county, there to be detained until the time fixed for trial as aforesaid. And on the day appointed for the trial, such fugitive, if committed to jail, shall be brought before said judge, or in case of his absence, sickness, or inability to attend, before some other judge of a court of record of this state residing within such county, by the written order of such judge, directed to the sheriff or jailer of the proper county, for final hearing and adjudication; and in case there shall be a breach of the condition of either of said bonds, the claimant shall have a right of action thereon, and recover as in other cases; and on said trial, either party shall be entitled to be heard by counsel, and shall have compulsory process to compel the attendance of witnesses.

Sect. V. It shall be the duty of the said judge, at the time to which the case is postponed as aforesaid, to proceed to hear the parties, and if it shall be proven to his satisfaction that the party arrested does owe labor or service to the claimant, he shall give such claimant, his or her agent or attorney, a certificate of that fact, which shall be a sufficient authority for such claimant, his or her agent or attorney to remove such fugitive from the state: but no such certificate shall be deemed a sufficient authority for the removal of such fugitive, unless the official character of the officer giving the same be duly authenticated, according to the provisions of this act in relation to the issuing of warrants. And if the party thus arrested shall not appear, according to the conditions of his or her bond, it shall be the duty of said judge to deliver the same to the claimant, his or her agent or attorney, to enable him or her to bring suit thereon.

Sect. VI. If any person or persons in this state shall counsel, advise, or entice any other person, who, by the laws of any other state, shall owe labor or service to any other person or persons, to leave, abandon, abscond or escape from the person or persons to whom such labor or service, according to the laws of such other state, is or may be due, or shall furnish money or conveyance of any kind, or any other facility, with intent and for the purpose of enabling such person, owing labor or service as aforesaid, to escape from or elude the claimant of such person, owing labor or service as aforesaid, knowing such person or persons to owe labor or service as aforesaid, every person so offending shall, upon conviction thereof by indictment, be fined in any sum not exceeding five hundred dollars, or be imprisoned in the jail of the county not exceeding sixty days, at the discretion of the court; and shall moreover be liable in an action at the suit of the party injured.

Sect. VII. If any person or persons shall falsely, fraudulently, and without proper authority, give to any other person, who, by the laws of any other state, shall owe labor or service to any person or persons, any certificate or other testimonial of emancipation, with the intent to defraud the person or persons to whom such labor or service may be due, knowing such person to owe labor or service as aforesaid; or shall harbor or conceal any such person owing labor or service as aforesaid, who may come into this state without the consent of the person or persons to whom such labor or service may be due, knowing such person to owe labor or service as aforesaid, every person so offending shall, upon conviction thereof by indictment, be fined in any sum not exceeding five hundred dollars, or be imprisoned in the jail of the county not exceeding sixty days, at the discretion of the court; and shall moreover be liable in an action at the suit of the party injured.

Sect. VIII. Any sheriff, or constable, who shall execute any process directed and delivered to him under the provisions of this act, or any clerk of a court, or mayor, who shall authenticate any certificate or warrant under the provisions of this act, shall receive the same fees as are now allowed by law for similar services in other cases.

Sect. IX. It shall be the duty of all officers proceeding under this act, to recognize, without proof, the existence of slavery or involuntary servitude, in the several states of this union, in which the same may exist or be recognized by law.

Sect. X. If any person, in any deposition or affidavit, or other oath or affirmation, taken pursuant to the provisions of this act, shall willfully and corruptly depose, affirm, or declare any matter to be fact, knowing the same to be false; or shall, in like manner, deny any matter to be fact, knowing the same to be true, every person so offending shall be deemed guilty of perjury, and, upon conviction thereof, shall be imprisoned in the penitentiary, and kept at hard labor not more than seven, nor less than three years.

Sect. XI. If any person or persons shall in any manner attempt to carry out of this state, or knowingly be aiding in carrying out of this state, any person, without first obtaining sufficient legal authority for so doing, according to the laws of this state or of the United States, every person so offending shall be deemed guilty of a misdemeanor, and upon conviction thereof shall be imprisoned in the penitentiary, and kept at hard labor, not less than three, nor more than seven years.

Sect. XII. That the fourth section of an act to regulate black and mulatto persons, passed January 5, 1804, and so much of the second section of the act to prevent kidnapping. passed February 15, 1831, as is inconsistent with the provisions of this act, be and the same is hereby repealed.

Sect. XIII. That a trial and judgment under the act of congress, entitled "an act respecting fugitives from justice, and persons escaping from the service of their masters," approved February 12, 1793, or a trial and judgment under the provisions of this act, shall be adjudged a final bar to any subsequent proceeding against such fugitive under the provisions of this act.

Sect. XIV. This act to take effect from and after the first day of May next. Passed February 26, 1839. Took effect May 1, 1839.

The 1839 Fugitive Slave Law certainly was a turning point in Ohio history and the highwater mark of the influence of the Slave Power in Ohio. The Law was not designed to simply supplement or tweak legal procedures regarding fugitive slaves. Rather, the Law—and associated resolutions in the 37th General Assembly—obviously were intended to crush Ohio's abolitionist movement. All you need do to see is read the Law. It was an existential threat, not only to fugitive slaves and free blacks, but also to the abolitionist movement itself because the Law made illegal virtually every abolitionist action regarding fugitive slaves.

Setting the Stage: The Second Trial
CHAPTER EIGHT

It was mid-April, 1839, and already John Bennington Mahan of Sardinia, Ohio, was trying to blindly find his way through a depressingly dark, narrow tunnel toward some semblance of bright white light. So far this year, he had lost an irreplaceable political ally, U.S. Sen. Thomas Morris (Dr. Beck's uncle), and Morris was replaced by an ardent anti-abolitionist, Benjamin Tappan. Mahan's petition for reimbursement in Columbus regarding losses suffered while spending more than two months in prison went nowhere. His health was poor. He also had been dragged through a Kentucky "kangaroo" court five months prior and, though not guilty, still had a spendy civil case hanging over his head. (The civil trial originally was supposed to begin in May, but he was trying to move that later.) He had worries about lawyer fees. He had worries about preparing for his civil trial.

The Ohio Fugitive Slave Law would take effect May 1 and carried enforceable, substantial penalties. He constantly worried about his "railroad" friends, especially in Sardinia or at Gist Settlement, and of their lives being regularly harassed or, as in the case of Gist Settlement, of his black friends there potentially being illegally kidnapped into slavery. He worried about Kentucky slave hunters harassing family and friends.

He also worried about fugitives, and how the new law could steal their courage to cross the wide Ohio River. Of course, he had a wife and family to feed, good children to love. He also had to live in Sardinia, the same village where two residents living near him allegedly had been eager to testify against him. And lastly, the Slave Power now knew better who he was, the names of abolitionist friends, how he operated, and even *when* he operated.

It was then Mahan realized *The Philanthropist* had been publishing his name as the Sardinia "agent" for acquiring subscriptions to the abolitionist newspaper, and *The Philanthropist* had published membership totals for the Sardinia Anti-Slavery Society listing his name as leader. Any anti-abolitionist Kentuckian with access to this Cincinnati newspaper could read how active he had been. *The Philanthropist* on October 4, 1838, reported his local anti-slavery society had eighty-four members. He had a target on his back.

Mahan had much to absorb. What happened next only put that much more on his plate, at a time when he should have been diligently preparing for a Maysville civil trial. The shenanigans, harassment, violence, and eventually, the *horrible murder*, began April 7 and would end weeks later.

On Sunday April 7, Tom Fox, a free black who lived at Gist Settlement and made barrels for a living, watched as five strange men approached on horseback. They all were from Arnheim and gave off a strange vibe. Under pretense of needing privacy to ask Fox to do work for them, they lured him into nearby trees, threatened him with death should he scream, tied him to a tree, and brought out irons to secure him. A neighboring elderly white woman heard Fox scream and ran over. She demanded the five strangers release him. Suddenly, as if on cue, a horseback group comprising of one white man and a handful of blacks rode into the woods, took control of the situation, freed Fox, and demanded the strangers present evidence of legal authority for restraining Fox. The strangers mounted horse and galloped off.

A week later, again on a Sunday, the initial five riders from Arnheim appeared along with a half-dozen helpers. The leader queried for Moses Cumberland, who wasn't home but could be found at church. One of this group, who happened to be a constable, Valentine Carberry, waved around an arrest warrant during a worship service for all to see, one that charged Cumberland with assault on two of the men from the prior Sunday. The arrest attempt and the way it was done caused an immediate uprising at Cumberland's church. Congregants punched and pushed back. One congregant exited out a door and rode to Sardinia to tell Mahan, and he rode there in response, along with Amos Pettijohn, Joseph Pettijohn, and maybe a dozen other Sardinians. They eventually spotted the posse holding Cumberland, and also the black Gist men who were chasing them. A significant altercation ensued.

On Monday April 15, next morning, Brown County deputies placed under arrest John B. Mahan, the Pettijohns, Dr. Beck, and Robert Huggins for disturbing the peace and assaulting Carberry and a posse member, Grant Lindsey. Mahan and the Pettijohns were released on bond for a trial scheduled September 30. The others were freed for lack of evidence.

That wasn't all. On Sunday April 21, a similar group of riders appeared once again at Gist Settlement before leaving. They were looking for, but had not found, various black men involved in the Cumberland and Fox fights.

A final—and this a *deadly*—altercation happened April 30, when another posse, this time of about twenty men, and having a warrant, tried arresting Jacob Cumberland, brother of Moses. Sally Hudson, John Hudson's sister, tried protecting Jacob. This time, Mahan and his Sardinia abolitionist friends were not around. A gunshot rang out.

Dr. Isaac Beck later wrote about this sequence of events that ended in murder. The ensuing legal maneuverings in Georgetown, which occurred the same summer as Mahan's second trial involving some of the same men but for a different incident, featured yet another run-in with attorney Thomas L. Hamer, the man who had given Beck his first job years earlier at Hamer's newspaper. Beck wrote:

> In [April] 1839, a negro named Tom Fox came to the [Gist Settlement] near here and loitered for some time. Some drunken loafers from around Arnheim, Ohio, (about five miles away) heard of him and one Sunday a gang of them came and seized him. The negroes made some opposition but (the loafers) tied Tom and they were about to leave when an old white lady named Sams, near whose house the seizure was made, heard the noise and came out to see what was going on. She found Tom tied, and ordered the blacks to untie him.
>
> (The blacks) having the old lady to back and encourage them, obeyed her, (and) the loafers (who were) intimidated by her presence retreated without Tom. And Tom did not loiter in the Camps much longer.
>
> A loafer's son, over their defeat, obtained a warrant for some offence I never heard what from a Justice of the Peace and a few days after a constable with a large posse returned and arrested Jacob Cumberland one of the blacks. The Constable and one of his posse were leading him with their arms around him very lovingly, lest the old man might escape, when Sally Hudson, a courageous black woman (and) a relative of the prisoner slipped up to them and seized one of their arms with her teeth. One of

the posse, James Kratzer, shot her in the back. At the shot, all left as fast as possible mounting the first horse he came to regardless of ownership.

Sally died in about two weeks. I made a post mortem and have the bullet yet. The ball had shattered one of the vertebrae and severed the spinal marrow.

We procured a warrant from the justice of the peace and had Kratzer arrested, he obtained (Thomas L.) Hamer, who "bulldozed" the Justice and he dismissed the murderer. We then succeeded in getting the case before the Grand Jury, but Hamer prevailed on the Judge (John W. Price) to send the witnesses for the defense before the grand jury. No indictment was found, and Kratzer is unpunished, except what Hamer inflicted, who got his farm for clearing him.

About that time, I have always been of the opinion there was a dozen or so of men in our County, if they had been assassinated in open day the murderers would never have been indicted.

Six weeks after having been freed on bail prior to his second trial and only a month after the Sally Hudson shooting, Mahan rode on horseback over two hundred miles to attend the fourth annual Ohio Anti-Slavery Society convention, held at Oberlin College, near Cleveland. Mahan personally addressed attendees. At least among abolitionists, he was well-respected for the personal sacrifices he had made, the character he had shown throughout his trial and in his letters, his Christian witness, and his rock-solid commitment to the cause. He was a positive example for other abolitionists to follow.

One Vermont newspaper account of the Ohio Anti-Slavery Society convention read: "John B. Mahan, an open-hearted, affable man, was present. He gave some facts in relation to himself. A prison was his abode for ten weeks. Most of the time he was manacled with twelve pounds of iron. His hands were at liberty, they feared less from his fists, than his feet. He was obliged to pay the jailor ten dollars for the privilege of seeing his friends! And, why all this? Ah, base man! He had assisted the poor in the name of the Lord.—On the trial it was not pretended, that he had personally been in Kentucky, but in a kind of mystical or ideal manner; only visible to the keen optics of Kentucky patriarchs; or he was a criminal by proxy, as O'Connell was considered to be in Alabama, while the Atlantic happened to lie between the guilty man and the scene of his crimes.

"Soon after Mahan's arrest, Greathouse, whose property he was charge with feeding (what a crime!) offered to secure his release for $1700. The reply (from Mahan) was "I shall never give that." A few days later only $1400 was required. "What! Says Mahan, $300 in as many days! That is making money fast here in prison! Still, I demur.

"He continued to grow rich at this rate, till only $400 were demanded. "Can't give it," was [Mahan's] reply. "What will you give; not 25 cents!" Thus ended the negotiation. The suit on the civil process is still pending. He has already expended $1200. Greathouse is a despicable fellow. Some time ago he was prosecuted for stealing fifty dollars. By giving a lawyer a thousand dollars, sending one witness to St. Louis, another to Pittsburgh, and hiring a man to drown a third, he deprived himself of the privilege of enjoying the sunshine thro' iron grates."

Mahan heard in August a book compiling his Maysville trial had been published and was being sold throughout the nation. An August ad in *Rochester Freeman* (New York), as one example, read: "THIS is a very important document—great principles were involved in the case; and here the reader will find them clearly stated, ably argued, and decisively settled. The Judge in his charge and decision; and the counsel in the speeches, have gone over the whole ground; and hence, have given a great amount of important information, in respect to the case before them. This document should be spread far and wide. It will do much directly and indirectly for ABOLITION. It can be sent by mail, or by the quantity, in other ways. Will not our friends in New York, in Boston, in Philadelphia, Pittsburg, Utica, etc., and throughout our own State, send in their orders for this "TRIAL?" *Now is the time*, while the River remains open. Single copy—25 (cents). A considerable reduction to those who purchase *by the quantity*."

Predictably, Mahan's September 30 trial was a duel of sorts between old enemies and opposing attorneys: Thomas L. Hamer, and Thomas Morris, i.e., the anti-abolitionist and former Congressman who desperately had wanted to be a senator, and the abolitionist and former Ohio Supreme Court Justice who had just been ousted as a senator.

At trial, Valentine Carberry and Mahan had different versions of the story. Carberry claimed he was the victim, and he and his posse had been beaten by Gist Settlement churchgoers wielding wooden clubs, and that Mahan and his "bloodhounds of abolition" all had been armed with pistols. The Pettijohns encountered Carberry and his group, he claimed, and they allegedly used strong language inciting the blacks following the posse to become violent.

Valentine Carberry testified that Mahan had cursed the men of the posse for being Democrats and that Mahan had ordered the blacks to "whip" all the white men dead. Carberry also claimed Mahan had shown up with about *one hundred* men, including more than thirty blacks. (How Mahan could have assembled that many men on such short notice was not mentioned.) Carberry concluded Mahan and others had been inciting a riot, and that their freeing Cumberland had been a "violent" act.

Carberry's testimony must have seemed plausible and believable to the jury consisting of six Georgetown men. Mahan found a Sardinia witness who contradicted much of what Carberry said, but the jury believed, or wanted to believe, Carberry.

The trial ended October 4, and sentencing occurred October 11. Mahan and Joseph Pettijohn were each found guilty by a jury of their Brown County peers, ordered to pay $50 each and costs, and spend ten days in Brown County jail having only bread and water for nourishment. They would never spend even one day in Brown County jail, however. Mahan's legal team appealed. The Ohio Supreme Court quickly declared an "error" had been made related to jury selection.

This second trial involving Mahan made the rounds across the nation, too. Mahan received positive press from the usual sources, such as *The Philanthropist* and *The Liberator*, and other abolitionist-sympathetic newspapers, but was heavily criticized and even mocked in the Democrat and Southern press, as would be expected. They hit him really hard. But first, from *The Liberator*, which revealed the reason why Mahan won on appeal to the Ohio Supreme Court.

> The Ohio *Philanthropist* makes some astounding developments respecting the recent conviction of this

individual on the charge of being concerned in a riot. The complaint, it seems, had no other foundation than this—that Mr. Mahan met an officer with a colored man in custody, and suspecting him to be acting illegally, asked permission to see his warrant. Some colored people being present, and supposing it to be a case of kidnapping, were of course much excited, and one of them threw a stick at the officer. Although Mr. Mahan offered no violence himself, but reproved those who did, and even offered to assist the officer in the discharge of his duty, if he could show that he was acting legally, he was nevertheless indicted for participating in a riot! The means by which he was convicted will appear by the following extract from the Philanthropist. How beautifully these human governments operate!

The trial commenced on Monday, Sept. 30, when the presiding judge proceeded to lecture the jury as to the qualifications as jurors to sit on the case, and said, "If any of them were abolitionists, they were unfit to serve." He then proceeded to catechize them, individually, in order to purge out this hated leaven, so that "the inflexible administration of even-handed justice" might be meted out to Mr. Mahan. One of the jurors, by the name of Purdum, as intelligent and honest a man as the county yeomanry affords, was rejected after the following dialogue.

Judge—Have you heard a statement of this case from either of the parties?
Purdum—I have not.
Judge—Have you formed an opinion on the case?
Purdum—No, sir.
Judge—Are you an abolitionist?
Purdum—I do not belong to any society, but I believe their main principles are correct.

Objections were immediately raised, and Mr. Purdum was discharged from the jury box. Thus, obtaining what may strictly be termed a *packed* jury, it is not at all surprising that there was an entire unanimity among the jury in a verdict. The trial lasted until nearly Friday noon, October 4, being closed on the part of the State by Mr. Hamer. This gentleman [Mr. Hamer] will be recollected by our readers as possessing a very tender conscience, and being scrupulously nice in refusing to issue a writ of habeas corpus, when Mr. M. [Mahan] was dragged to a Kentucky prison by the perjury of Greathouse and his confederates. The jury, on their oaths, declared a verdict of "guilty" against J.B. Mahan for a regular built riot. Even the judge himself seemed taken by surprise. "What," he exclaimed, "on *all* the counts!" "Yes," was the reply. "So say you all, gentlemen?" "Yes," was the response.

We understand that a bill of exceptions was filed by the defendant, but they were overruled by the Court. An appeal was then taken to the Supreme Court, at which tribunal the case will be re-adjudicated.

Mahan, by this time, was a man loved or hated—as are most people who push societal envelopes. The negative press following his arrest and conviction came heavy-handed and mean, unlike after his first trial when many people, even many anti-abolitionists, saw him as a victim.

The first negative press came from the Democrat-leaning *Ohio Statesman* of Columbus. (Thomas L. Hamer may have sent the letter to the editor mentioned below, given how he had sent a similar letter to the *Ohio Statesman* after refusing to produce a writ of habeas corpus for Mahan the prior year. If so, Hamer seemed to be doing everything he could to undermine Mahan, while enhancing his own party and himself. This article was republished in the *Wilmington Democrat and Herald*.)

ABOLITION RIOT

The following extract from a letter to the editor, dated Georgetown, Brown County, April 15th, gives an account of one of the most disgraceful transactions that has occurred in a long time. We will not comment upon it.

The *facts* are sufficient to arouse the public indignation: A most disgraceful affair occurred near Georgetown, or rather Sardinia, on Saturday 14th inst. A negro residing in or near the camps, had assaulted an individual and had been arrested by a constable, who was proceeding to take him before a magistrate, to have him tried for the violation of the laws.

After the constable had proceeded a short distance, a band of desperadoes, headed by the notorious John B. Mahan, armed with pistols and clubs, rescued the negro from the hands of the officer of the law, and set him at liberty. Thus, you see the effects of the accursed doctrine of abolitionism. The laws of the State are set at open defense in broad daylight, on the sabbath, and that, too, a minister of the gospel!! A minister of the gospel heads a mob, and tramples under their unhallowed feet the laws of their country. Such conduct deserves universal condemnation by every friend of good order of society. "They will all, I suppose, be arrested and brought to trial; and I hope, if it can be, sent to the penitentiary. Such men ought not to be permitted longer to remain in civilized society."

From the *Urbana Democrat and Herald*:

Rev. John B. Mahan.—This notorious individual was convicted in conjunction with one or two others at the late sitting of the Court of Common Pleas for Brown County, of a riot in rescuing a negro man from the hands of a constable some time since; and sentenced to pay a fine of $50 and be imprisoned in the dungeon of the jail of that county for ten days, and fed bread and water....Security was however obtained and an appeal taken to the Supreme Court, through the intervention of the attorneys for the defense—where doubtless he will have *justice meted out to him*.

From the *Cleveland Weekly Plain Dealer*:

"Honesty is the best policy."
Rev. John B. Mahan, Joseph Pettijohn, and Amos Pettijohn, who were indicted by the Grand Jury of Brown County, for a riot, in rescuing a negro from the hands of a constable, had their trial last week, before the Court of Common Pleas, of that county, and found GUILTY of the charge brought against them in the indictment. The two formers, Mahan, and Joseph Pettijohn, were sentenced to pay a fine of fifty dollars each, to be imprisoned in the dungeon of the jail of Brown County for ten days, and fed on bread and water only, and to pay the cost of prosecution. We have copied from the Statesman an account of the trial before the Court, which will be found in another column. May it prove a warning to evil doers.

The *Cleveland Daily Herald* had this to opine:

In pronouncing sentence upon them, the presiding Judge, in a brief and impressive address to the prisoners, dwelt upon the enormity of the offence, and admonished them to behave for the future as quiet and peaceable citizens. He reminded Mahan, that it had been proved on the trial that he was a Minister of the Gospel of Peace; that the riot had taken place on the Sabbath day; that, instead of attending the duties of his sacred calling, he had been found traversing the country and resisting a ministerial officer in the regular discharge of his duties.

He advised him, that his present situation should be a warning to him, not to allow his excessive Philanthropy, either for the BLACK or the white race, to lead him into similar aggressions hereafter. During this time, those who saw him, say that his countenance, which before had been bold and confident, seemed to fall under the just reproof administered from the Court.

Once again, the name "John B. Mahan" and "abolitionist" appeared in print nationwide, with this as a sampling: *Rochester Freeman* (N.Y.), *Vermont Telegraph*, *Western Citizen* (Ky.), *The Record* (Penn.), *The Washington Union* (D.C.), *Richmond Enquirer* (Va.), *Pittsburgh Post-Gazette*, *Huntsville Democrat* (Ala.), *Philadelphia Inquirer*, *Kennebec Journal* (Me.), *The Buffalo Commercial*, *Vermont Phoenix*, *Hartford Courant* (Conn.), and *Baltimore Sun*.

As for the latter, *The Baltimore Sun* opined October 22 regarding the verdict: "This disposition to do justice is all that is requisite, to gain the confidence of the south, for those States whose institutions differ from theirs in regards to point—that of domestic slavery; and will do more for the eradication of that evil than all the efforts of a wild fanaticism."

Setting the Stage: The Third Trial
CHAPTER NINE

John B. Mahan spent many days over the next year becoming personally involved in preparing his own defense in his civil trial against Greathouse in Maysville. Greathouse wanted more than a thousand dollars in compensation for losing two slaves. Mahan did not want to pay him even "25 cents."

Mahan personally in 1839-40 deposed over sixty people, including ten reputable Northern Ohioans who had known Perrigo in Huron County, not far from Lake Erie, who all claimed Perrigo was a "notorious gambler, swindler, and horse-racer." Perrigo had even scammed Sandusky citizens over the building of the Milan Canal. Mahan had done the legwork himself to save precious money, and in that vein would represent himself at his trial. It was a risky move.

The civil trial rolled around, finally, in spring 1841, at the same exact courthouse in Maysville, Kentucky, as the first. Greathouse brought in a deposition from a surprising witness, an Ann Devore, who claimed she had been a local schoolteacher and tenant of Mahan, and who allegedly had overheard many conversations in which she had heard Mahan had hidden the slaves at his home and paid them five dollars before sending them off to Canada.

For nearly every witness or bizarre claim originating from Greathouse's camp, Mahan had a prepared answer, including one deposition from a free black man who personally had escorted the slave Nelson (one of two Greathouse fugitives) from Georgetown to Sicily and on to Wilmington, completely bypassing Mahan's Sardinia home.

Political hay was made in the early 2020s concerning the practice of "lawfare," which could be defined as trying to embarrass, intimidate, harass, and bankrupt an innocent opponent through legal means. If this was Greathouse's purpose, then he was doing a superb job.

The Cincinnati Enquirer on June 1, 1841, announced Mahan's civil suit fate, reprinting an article from the *Maysville Eagle*. It read: "A Righteous Verdict.—Mr. William Greathouse, of this county at the present term of the Mason Circuit court, obtained a verdict against Rev. John B. Mahan, for $1600, the value of two negro men, which Mahan enticed away from the service of the former in [1838], and sent on to Canada. It will be recollected, it was for this same offence that Mahan was brought to Kentucky in [1838], by the requisition of the Governor, but for want of jurisdiction in the Court, escaped being sent to penitentiary. If the abolitionists were made to pay more frequently in this way, for their villainous depredations upon the property of Kentucky citizens, it would soon put an end to the practice of negro stealing, carried to such an infamous extent of late by them."

John was crushed. He could not understand how truth had not won out. He had spent more than a year gathering evidence. He had prayed, and prayed. He had the prayers of all his friends working on his behalf. At times, he felt as if the Lord had forsaken him. *But why? Oh Lord, what am I going to do?* It grated him that perjurers like Perrigo and Greathouse could repeatedly lie in court and get away with it. Then he realized his Lord had gone through something similar. John couldn't get the ending of Psalm 44 off his heart.

Awake, Lord! Why do you sleep?
Rouse yourself! Do not reject us forever.
Why do you hide your face and forget our misery and oppression?
We are brought down to the dust; our bodies cling to the ground.
Rise up and help us; rescue us because of your unfailing love.

A number of newspaper accounts of the civil case could be brought forward. Most were negative for Mahan. But the below account originated with John's closest abolitionist friends, who came to his defense, and it was published in the *National Anti-Slavery Standard* for national consumption. At least with his abolitionist brethren reading about his plight he could get a sympathetic audience and potentially the last word on the Greathouse matter. His friends rigorously laid out the backstory of what they proclaimed as the truth behind Mahan's first, third, and fourth trials. Let the reader be the judge.

> THE WHOLE CASE OF JOHN B. MAHAN
> At a meeting of the Sardinia Anti-Slavery Society, held June 3d 1841, the following resolutions were passed unanimously:
> Whereas, we understand that the Mason Circuit Court, Kentucky, has recently decided the cause of Wm. Greathouse vs. John B. Mahan, by rendering judgment against the defendant for sixteen hundred dollars with interest and cost of suit: therefore,
> Resolved, That we consider that decision as a gross perversion of justice, and an iniquitous violation of the rights of man, done in obedience to the mandate of slavery.

Resolved, That such perversion of right should be held up to the world for public reprobation:—therefore,

Resolved, That a committee of five be appointed to make out a statement of the facts in the above cause, and report them to this Society at some subsequent meeting, for examination and revision, for the purpose of this publication.

Resolved, That the committee consists of the following persons: Dr. I.M. Beck, J.E. Huggins, Josiah Moore, James Cumberland and Lewis Pettijohn.

On motion, adjourned to meet Monday, 14th inst. at 7 o'clock, PM.

Monday evening, June 14th the Society met agreeably to adjournment: whereupon the committee appointed to report the facts in relation to the case of Wm. Greathouse vs. J.B. Mahan, presented the following report, which was received and unanimously adopted:

Your committee to whom was referred the case of the law suit which was recently decided in the Mason Circuit Court, in the State of Kentucky, between Wm. Greathouse of Mason County, Kentucky, and John B. Mahan, of the State of Ohio, after a patient investigation and mature reflection on the subject, as leave to report as follows:

Wm. Greathouse, by the procurement of Jas. Rock, alias Jas. Rock Perrigo, a strolling gambler and horse racer, a most infamous swindler, as is clearly established, partly by his cross-examination, and in part by ten depositions of the most respectable gentlemen in Huron County, did by the foulest perjury at the Mason Circuit Court, August term, 1838, cause the said J.B. Mahan to be indicted in two indictments, charging him with aiding and assisting two slaves, (John and Nelson) the property of William Greathouse, to escape out of beyond the State of Kentucky; whereupon Mr. Clark, Governor of Kentucky, made a requisition of the Governor of Ohio, Jos. Vance, to deliver over to his agent the said J. B. Mahan as a fugitive from justice, notwithstanding the said J.B. Mahan had not been within the jurisdiction of said Court for nineteen years and a half, and had not at any time had any correspondence with any person residing there.

According to the said requisition, said J.B. Mahan was delivered over to the agent of Governor Clark, and imprisoned in the Mason County jail for more than ten weeks.

On the second day of his imprisonment, a capias was served on him in person, by the sheriff of the county, to answer unto William Greathouse in damages in the sum on $1700, the value of said slaves. On the next day after his arrest on the capias, overtures were sent into the prison for a compromise of the whole matter, criminal and civil—Greathouse proposing, that if the value of said negroes should be left with some responsible person in Ohio, he would send the witness Perrigo out of the way at court, and so the said J.B. Mahan should be acquitted.

J.B. Mahan feeling a consciousness of innocence, and that none of his actions had made him liable for the value of said slaves, utterly refused a compromise on any conditions whatever. Greathouse continued from time to time to send in overtures. He also sent overtures to said Mahan's family by the Rev. John Meek, his friend in Ohio, but finding every effort to obtain pay for his fugitive slaves in that way utterly fruitless, he left off his importunities, and commenced making preparations to convict Mahan of the offence for which he stood indicted.

In order to do this, he employed four able lawyers, and when court came on, by means of these and his mercenary witness Perrigo, he thought to make sure work; but in this was sadly foiled. Said Mahan was acquitted; the testimony of said Perrigo, though absolutely a perjury, not being of such a kind as to give the court jurisdiction in the case.

The said Greathouse then made another effort at obtaining a compromise of the suit for damages, for the value of said negroes. He introduced himself to Mr. Mahan, brother of J.B. Mahan, who was then at Washington [Maysville], and offered by him to take $800, and compromise the suit: but not succeeding in this, and beginning to think it a desperate case, he had the suit put off till the next term, hoping in the mean time to find some testimony that might subserve the interests of his suit.

He procured an individual who resides in Sardinia, by bribery or other means, to go to Kentucky and give his deposition, in which he set forth that he saw the slaves John and Nelson at the house of J.B. Mahan, in Sardinia, Ohio, and saw the said Mahan give one of them monies. He also prevailed on Ann A. Devore, a strolling woman in the county of Brown, and State of Ohio, to go south to the mouth of the Ohio River, that he might there take her deposition without subjecting her to a prosecution for perjury.

She there, at Cairo, Illinois, swore that in 1838 at the time said slave ran away, she was boarding at the tavern house of J.B. Mahan, and teaching school in the neighborhood; and that she saw the said Wm. Greathouse at said Mahan's, hunting his negroes; and that said Mahan had his negroes upstairs, and so secreted them there for eight or ten days, then gave them a five dollar bill and sent them on their way to Canada.

All of which said Mahan proved to be false by more than a score of witnesses. And had her deposition been made in Brown County, nothing could have saved her from a conviction of perjury, and imprisonment in the penitentiary. The fact, that she did not board at the tavern of J.B. Mahan in the summer of 1838, and teach a school in the neighborhood of Sardinia, are so permanently notorious accounts for the fact that she could not be induced to give such testimony till she was out of the jurisdiction of an Ohio Court.

Greathouse repeatedly offered to hire her (according to her own statement) to swear, while she resided in Brown County. But all to no purpose, she knowing the great peril to which she would expose herself by the commission of such a perjury.

J.B. Mahan, in his defense at a very considerable cost, and great loss of time, obtained the testimony of ten of the most respectable men at Norwalk and Milan, Huron County, Ohio, by which he showed to the court and jury that J.R. Perrigo was a most infamous gambler, swindler, and horse-racer; that he and his associates (one of whom was afterwards shot by a Kentuckian at Sandusky city, in an affray) carried on a series of swindling transactions on the Milan canal, in 1834, and swindled several citizens of that county out of not less than twenty thousand dollars' worth of goods, wares, merchandise, horse and more; that he was indicted in Huron County and fled; he afterwards engaged, according to his own confession, (see cross examination) in horse-racing.

He also took more than sixty depositions in Brown County, of men and women of the most respectable standing in society, both abolitionists and anti-abolitionists, by which he clearly and sufficiently proved the following facts:

1st. That Ann A. Devore's testimony was all false. That she did not board at the tavern of J.B. Mahan, and keep a school in the neighborhood of Sardinia in 1838, at the time said slaves, John and Nelson, ran away; that she is a woman of infamous character, and not worthy of credit.

2d. That the slave John came to Sardinia in the morning, and stayed publicly through the day; was not secreted nor concealed—that a Mr. Lewis Pettijohn invited him in the evening to go with him to his residence in Highland County, and that a certain J.W.J. Myers took two horses and assisted the said John on his way towards Canada— that J.B. Mahan had nothing to do with facilitating the escape of said [slave] John.

3d. That a certain colored man named Vieny, found the said Nelson escaping at a point near Georgetown, Brown County, Ohio, and took him to a certain A. Huggins, not coming within four miles of Sardinia; and that a certain J.B. Huggins, now residing at Quincy, Illinois, took horses and assisted the said Nelson to Wilmington, Clinton County, Ohio. Consequently, he was never nearer Sardinia than four miles; and that said J.B. Mahan knew nothing of the said Nelson or his escape, till he was 40 miles north of his residence.

4th. That the whole of said Mahan's offence, in relation to the said slaves John and Nelson, consisted principally in giving the said John entertainment at his table for the space of one day, and that in the most public manner. These proofs, together with others of minor importance, being submitted to the jury in the Mason Circuit Court, May term, 1841, the jury returned a verdict for the plaintiff for the value of said John and Nelson—$1600 damages. These are the most prominent facts of the case, from which we think may be clearly drawn the following deductions.

1st. That Wm. Greathouse, whatever might have been the intentions of aiders and abettors, had no other design in procuring the delivery of J.B. Mahan to the authorities of Kentucky, than to subserve his own pecuniary interests, by having the defendant brought within slaveholding jurisdiction, that he might have the advantage of a slaveholding court and jury—the advantage of the defendant and witnesses' residence in another State. And the vent shows that he did not err in his calculations on the vigilance of the slave power, to protect its interest by warping the judgment of court and jury.

2d. That Gov. Vance of Ohio, in issuing his warrant for the delivery over of said defendant, for an act merely *malum prohibitum*, acted every way unworthy of the trust reposed in him as Governor of a free and independent State. That in delivering over fugitives from justice, according to the provisions of the constitution of the U.S., the crime set forth in the requisition should be *malum in se* [wrong in itself], such an act as is pronounced criminal by the laws and religions of all civilized countries, and in the second place should be free from a fraudulent of suspicious circumstances

3d. That as the requisition of Gov. Clark for the delivery over of the defendant, bore on the very face of it a falsehood of the foulest sort, which consisted in averring that the defendant had fled from justice, away from Mason County, Kentucky, while at the same time neither the perjured witness, the grand jury who found the indictment, the prosecutor, nor his assistants, nor any other person, ever pretended that the defendant had ever been in the State of Kentucky at any time previous to his arrest, is a circumstance quite sufficient to justify the Governors of Ohio, in all their future course, in relation to demands of a similar kind coming from that quarter, to be exceedingly cautious, and to deliver over persons claimed as fugitives from justice, only after the defendant is brought before the Governor, and permitted to show any fraud which may exist in his case.

4th. That notwithstanding several witnesses, especially Ann A. Devore, J.R. Perrigo, and the individual who resides in Sardinia, whose name we spare, committed perjury of the most iniquitous character; still their testimony was so fully confronted by scores of witnesses of the most respectable standing, that nothing but the strongest bias on a slaveholding jury and slaveholding court, in favor of slavery and against liberty, would have procured a verdict in favor of the plaintiff.

5th. That henceforth so long as slavery exists, abolitionists and all philanthropists living on its borders, who are known publicly to exercise the hospitality of the Bible towards the needy, stand in jeopardy every hour, and are eminently in danger of being grievously harassed with lawsuits of the most unjust kind.

6th. That unless this, and like cases, receive the reprobation which they deserve from the public, no man in the free States will be secure one hour: for slaveholders will find it cheaper to recover the price of their fugitive by commencing a prosecution against some respectable individual (through whose neighborhood he passed) and have him brought within the jurisdiction of a pro-slavery court, and there establish his claim by perjured witnesses, than to hire mercenaries to hunt his fugitives. It will cost less to hire men to commit the necessary perjury, than to catch the fugitive. For very few who will do the last, but will cheerfully do the first.

Resolved, That the resolutions of the last meeting of this Society, relating to the business of the present meeting, together with the report of the committee, be forwarded to the *Philanthropist* for publication.

For what it was worth, Mahan was the table talk of a nation once again, with the *Charleston Daily Courier, Daily Selma Reporter, Vermont Watchman, Baltimore Sun, Mississippi Free Trader, New York Evening Post, Philadelphia Inquirer,*

National Anti-Slavery Standard (New York) and a host of other major newspapers noting he had lost $1600 in a civil suit. He had done everything he could to win that case. He hoped his children would not doubt his innocence because he had repeatedly told them he had not sinned. In a way, by standing up to the Slave Power, he had suffered a similar fate as Sen. Thomas Morris, who had lost his U.S. Senate seat because of being an ardent abolitionist. You could say the same for Elijah Lovejoy, who literally lost his life fighting for abolition. *Praise God for them, he thought.*

Setting the Stage: The Final Years
CHAPTER TEN

Mahan and his Sardinia co-laborers did not waste any time getting back to business after the civil suit ended. The unfairness of the process hardened Mahan's resolve once more. He realized what had happened could repeat itself. The Ohio Fugitive Slave Law of 1839 was suffocating. A direction on how to move the just cause of abolition forward had become clear to him after the last trial, i.e., from not only changing hearts and minds through moral persuasion, and doing the physical work of an abolitionist, but also to become more involved in politics at all levels.

Although having some sympathy and supporters inside the Whig camp, the Whigs and Vance had disappointed him. Many Democrats had tried to destroy him. For an immediate abolitionist who operated on principle, the only alternative to the above seemed the Liberty Party and its candidate James G. Birney.

Just two months after the civil trial ended, the Sardinia Anti-Slavery Society convened to move forward. It was great personally for Mahan to refocus, get back on point, and work through his troubles. He loved these men like brothers. They enjoyed having him back. They had been with him through thick and thin and had assisted so much over the prior three tumultuous years. He also enjoyed having a black man, James Cumberland, in the Society.

According to Dr. Beck, wealthy abolitionists covered Mahan's attorney fees for the first trial, and William Dunlap of Ripley took care of the bond for the third. Mahan received help from friends and family. He also did his own leg work for the third trial, even going to Northern Ohio to depose witnesses, and represented himself at court. While he was doing all this trial work he could not work and earn a living. Mahan was in a poor financial state. The letter below ran in the *Oberlin Evangelist* in August 1841, written by James Shaw, a Presbyterian pastor.

TO THE FRIENDS OF THE SLAVE IN OHIO

Two or three weeks since, I saw in the *Philanthropist*, an article headed, "The whole case detailed," respecting the persecutions, imprisonment, and consequent pecuniary embarrassment of our brother and fellow-laborer JOHN B. MAHAN. Perhaps that statement of the case, which I *know* to be true in every particular, is sufficient to awaken in his behalf that *peculiar* kind of sympathy which his circumstances require. "It seems good to me," however, "having had a perfect understanding of all things" relating to the case from the first—having been a member of Mahan's family for more than two years, the last past—to make this appeal to the friends of the oppressed in Ohio, in his behalf. I ask your assistance for the following reasons:

[First]: The burden Mahan has been called to bear is heavy, and we are commanded to "bear one another's burdens." The expenses he has incurred in his legal defense, with the costs and damages, which have been assessed upon him by the court, amount to between two and three thousand dollars. Some assistance has been received, but a very large part of the burden is still resting upon Mahan and the gentleman who kindly entered bonds with him for whatever costs and damages might be assessed in the issue of the case. He has also suffered other losses, considerable, which might have been avoided had he not been taken away from his business.

[Second]: Mr. Mahan's family is large, his property rather small, and somewhat embarrassed. Without assistance, he must be homeless and penniless.

[Third]: *The case is really our own.* The charge of kidnapping, on which Mahan was delivered up to the Kentucky authorities was a mere *pretense*, as may be seen by a reference to the published pleadings on the trial, for the sake of obtaining a decision on the question: "*Can a man commit a crime where he is not?*" Leading men in Mason County said, before the trial, that Mahan was "selected," not because he was more guilty, or even as guilty as many others in Ohio, but because in his case they thought there was more probability, than in any other, of obtaining such a decision as they wished. With such a decision in their favor, they expected to make every person in Ohio, who might extend any form of assistance to fugitives from Kentucky oppression, liable in their own courts for the price of every such fugitive.

On the charge of kidnapping, it was the duty of the prosecuting attorney, and whoever might be associated with him in business, to manage the case and plead against Mahan. But additional counsel was *employed and paid*—not by Greathouse, whose slaves Mahan was charged with having kidnapped—*but by the Slaveholders of Mason County.* The trial then was one in which SLAVERY, in the persons of the Slaveholders of Mason County, was the plaintiff; and those in Ohio, who feel it to be their duty and privilege to aid such as are fleeing from the face of the spoiler, in the person of J.B. Mahan, were the defendants. Let us then promptly and cheerfully pay the expenses of a suit, which was instituted upon the denial of some of our religious rights and privileges; and the prosecuted for the purpose of entrapping *us* in the snare of oppression to be punished, if we should dare to act in accordance with those rights and privileges.

Will not every friend of the slave in Ohio say, it is enough, and more than sufficient, that Mahan should be torn away from his family, chained, and incarcerated ten weeks, all the while not knowing that he should ever see home and friends again? Whatever sacrifice of property is called for in the case, we ask the privilege of making?

Those who wish to contribute can send their contributions by mail. Mr. Mahan's address is Sardinia, Brown Co., Ohio—JAMES SHAW.

Virtually the same week the *Oberlin Evangelist* helped make a direct plea to aid Mahan, the article below appeared in the *Georgetown Democratic Standard*. Mahan's political boxing gloves were off. He was ready to brawl. Yet his health was not cooperating.

ABOLITION MEETING

At a Meeting of Anti-Slavery voters, held at Sardinia on the thirteenth instant. The following resolutions were unanimously adopted.

Whereas, three millions of our countrymen, without having forfeited their rights to liberty by the commission of any crime, together with their offsprings for all time to come, are destined by the express statutes of the slaveholding states and also by the connivance and the direct and indirect action of the free States and to the General Government of the union to an unjust cruel and unrequited state of servitude,

Resolved, Therefore, 1st. That as an antislavery men we cannot consistently vote for any candidate for office in the Executive or Legislative department of our state or of the United States Government who does not hold in the language of the American bill of rights, that all men are endowed with certain inalienable rights, amongst which are life, liberty and the pursuits of happiness, and that it is a mean and contemptible evasion to say that a *black* man, a *red* man, or a *dusky* man is not a man, in the sense of the American bill of rights.

2nd. That we cannot vote for any candidate for the office of Senator or representative in the Ohio Legislature who will not do all in his power, to repeal the black laws of Ohio. The law requiring blacks and mulattoes to give resident white bail for their maintenance and good behavior before they are permitted to make a settlement in the state. That which taxes the blacks and mulattoes for the support of common school and at the same time prohibits them from participating in the advantages of said school.

The law that prohibits blacks and mulattoes from giving testimony in court of justice, when the interests of white persons may be affected; and especially the black acts of 1838-39 which recognize the right existence of slavery in their state, convert its ministerial officers into hunting dogs to catch fugitive slaves, and make it a penal offence to exercise the office of philanthropy and charity to an unoffending stranger.

3d. That we deeply deplore the disposition manifested by many abolitionists to care more for loaves and fishes for themselves than for liberty for those in bonds; to regard the present deranged state of the currency of the country, as a greater evil than the enslavement of three millions of our country-men. And we are constrained in the exercise of all charity, and good conscience, to regard all opposition to slavery that consists merely in thinking, and talking, and praying against slavery, without carrying out anti-slavery sentiments in course of corresponding actions and especially at the polls, to be hollow hearted hypocrisy.

4th. Resolved that although a great majority of us have generally voted with the Whigs, yet we regard the great principles involved in anti-slavery as paramount to any dollar and cent matters, bank or anti-bank questions, or any other subject of difference between Whigs and Democrats.

5th. Resolved that a committee of three persons be appointed by the chairman of this meeting to correspond with committees that may be appointed by the several counties composing this senatorial district on the subject of Independent Nominations.

6th. Resolved that the committee of correspondence named in the 5th Resolution are hereby authorized to call a meeting for this county, to nominate a suitable candidate for this county for Representative in the state Legislature; in case the Whigs or Democratic convention shall not bring out a suitable candidate.

7th. Resolved that a copy of the proceedings of this meeting, be forwarded to the Editors of the Philanthropist, Political Examiner, Democratic Standard and Ripley Telegraph for publication.

W. McCoy, Josiah Moore, and J.B. Mahan, were appointed the committee of correspondence.

I.M BECK, Chair. Josiah Moore, Sec'y.

A couple weeks later, on September 17, 1841, Mahan was on the road to nearby Batavia, in Clermont County, speaking and raising money for *The Philanthropist*. He opened the meeting with a prayer, and was appointed to a three-member committee to nominate a candidate for Ohio Senate covering Brown, Clermont, and Clinton Counties. They nominated John Jolliffe. On a motion by John B. Mahan, the meeting made the following resolution: "That the Philanthropist, and Dr. Bailey as its editor, must be sustained, and we exhort all our friends, at this particular time, to make extraordinary efforts to raise funds by contribution for that purpose. On motion, a contribution for the above purpose was taken at this meeting, and there was received $9.00."

The strategic move of Mahan's group of abolitionists having more of a political focus gelled in September 1842, when representatives from Brown, Clermont, and Clinton Counties met to nominate Liberty Party state legislature candidates. For state representative, they chose Josiah Moore and Alexander Campbell of Brown County, Benjamin Morris of Clermont County, and Absalom Douglass of Clinton County. They chose C.B. Huber of Clermont County for state senate. One resolution from this meeting, published in the *Georgetown Democratic Standard*, read: "Resolved, that the principles and conduct of both the great political parties are such as should deprive them of the support and confidence of every believer in the doctrines of the Declaration of Independence."

Mahan had seen how losing Thomas Morris and gaining a Democrat Ohio legislature and governor had damaged the abolitionist cause. He understood now, on a deeper level, the importance of having political power to accomplish good.

In much of 1843, Mahan spent a great deal of time on the road, like he had in Batavia, sometimes out of state, away from Polly and the kids, as a spokesperson for *The Philanthropist* and as a Liberty Party proponent. His close friend, James G. Birney, who had said nice things about him in 1835, would run for U.S. President on the Liberty Party ticket in 1844. His other close friend, former Senator Thomas Morris, who had been his attorney during the second trial, would run for U.S. Vice President on the Liberty Party ticket.

He saw political solutions. For example, one huge obstacle to abolitionists since 1839 that needed tearing down was the Ohio Fugitive Slave Law. Right from the get-go, the Law had been a flashpoint for abolitionists. About two months after enactment, the depth and breadth of the Law began hitting home to Ohioans. On July 18, 1839, a posse of eight men from Kanawha County, Virginia (West Virginia), arrived in Marion, Ohio, to claim "Black Bill" as a fugitive slave. They promptly arrested and jailed him in accordance with the new Ohio Fugitive Slave Law.

But Bill was an extremely popular figure throughout Marion. After fleeing his Virginia master, he had moved to Marion, and for the last year had been a laborer, butcher, barber, and fiddler. He was well-liked and a valued community member. He had made many white friends.

At trial in Marion on August 27, Judge Ozias Bowen ruled that a man by the last name of Van Bibber, Bill's alleged owner, who had brought a posse with him, had failed to prove ownership. Bowen learned a cousin of Van Bibber, John Lewis, had true ownership of "Black Bill" at the time of Bill's escape two years prior.

Seconds after Bowen announced, "The defendant is dismissed from custody," one of Van Bibber's seven "associates," McClanahan, grabbed Black Bill by the throat and squeezed. The claimant attorney declared his eight clients would be taking Black Bill back to Virginia in order to reunite him with John Lewis. The eight posse members "dragged and kicked (Bill) from the courtroom into the entry, downstairs, into the vestibule and courtyard and into the street."

The Virginians held the citizenry of Marion at bay until the citizenry raided the armory and returned bearing plenty of arms. It was a stand-off. Another local judge, Anderson, boldly marched up to the room where the Virginians held Black Bill and "pressed his way in, followed by others, ordered the men guarding Black Bill to release him, (and he, Anderson) burst the back door of the office open and Bill darted out." Bill ran towards Canada, followed by McClanahan, who nearly caught up with Bill until a young Quaker man tripped him. The Virginians were arrested and indicted for assault and battery, and for resisting the officers of the court.

Similar to Mahan, "Black Bill" made national news and, especially in Ohio, led to abolitionist and anti-abolitionist newspaper editors and politicians butting heads once again over the Ohio Fugitive Slave Law. For example, Marion anti-abolitionists called a meeting in February 1840. Abolitionists about the same time printed and distributed a handbill entitled, "Freedom of Speech." They held their own meeting. It was chaos like that in Marion that made the over-reaching Ohio Fugitive Slave Law unpopular, and gave abolitionists, like Mahan, an opportunity to further press their case for its repeal.

The Ohio Fugitive Slave Law was repealed January 19, 1843. Suddenly, the Sardinia abolitionists were able to operate at full strength again.

Setting the Stage: The Fourth Trial
CHAPTER ELEVEN

The years 1843-44 were painful for John Bennington Mahan. He was only in his early forties and his health problems were worsening. He probably had what doctors today call tuberculosis (TB), but to Mahan and Beck the lung disease was known as consumption. Doctors did not understand until the 1880s what caused "consumption," and so treated the disease in ways that would make modern medical professionals scratch heads.

Mahan "got" TB airborne through a bacterium-infected person. People can develop tuberculosis years after being exposed. The disease progresses through primary, latent, and active stages. According to Mayo Clinic, "Active TB (tuberculosis) disease may happen right after primary infection. But it usually happens after months or years of latent TB infection."

Symptoms of active TB can include cough, chest pain, coughing up blood, pain with breathing or coughing, chills, fever, weight loss, tiredness, and appetite loss. TB infection can spread out from the lungs and symptoms vary depending on body parts infected. TB can be a long-lasting, chronic disease. It would have been difficult for Mahan to function while having active TB. He sometimes felt as if he was too young to have his health be in such poor shape.

Claimed Mayo Clinic, "The disease is more likely to spread when people spend a lot of time together in an indoor space."

It has been speculated or perpetuated by some writers that Mahan passed away of TB caught while incarcerated two months in Mason County jail. Given most jail cells aren't packed with people—often they are set up for only one person—the likelihood of Mahan "getting" the TB bacterium in jail more so than in any other place would not seem likely. Perhaps more likely would have been that Mahan acquired the bacterium at a crowded abolitionist convention, a packed church meeting, or through spending time at his "Temperance Tavern" on a crowded day. Mahan also housed visitors at his "tavern" who could have passed on TB. In 1841, for example, in terms of visitors, Brown County even reimbursed Mahan for expenses related to housing Adam Bender, an "insane" person.

His first trial involved spending hours on end inside a packed *courtroom*, too. All he needed to be infected was have one infected person cough on him.

The healthcare treatment in the 1840s for TB, or "consumption," was unlike anything today, and may have worsened Mahan's health. Dr. Isaac Beck was most likely Mahan's doctor. If like most medical doctors of his day, Beck, for treatment, would have followed the writings and opinions of the late Dr. Benjamin Rush. It was Rush who believed tobacco smoking often caused TB, and that the best treatment options for TB were horseback riding, a meat-only diet, opium usage, bleeding, and purging.

Besides physical health, Mahan most certainly had some level of depression too, as strongly inferred by one author. This could have been not only due to his deteriorating physical condition, i.e., active TB symptoms and knowing death could be imminent, but also to several lamentable events. As we shall see, for Mahan not to be at all negatively affected by what happened to him in 1843-44 would have been nothing shy of a miracle. (Which was possible, of course.) He indeed was a strong man of faith, yet at the same time was a human being able to handle only so much.

For example, any depression could have started or been worsened by daughter Mary Jane passing away August 1843. Or by the brutal whipping July 1844 of a free black named Harbor Hurley fifteen miles from Sardinia; a band of vigilantes had accused Hurley of a crime but had no proof.

A depression could have been compounded by the 1844 presidential election—one Mahan had invested heart and soul in—in which his Liberty Party received but 2.3 percent of the national vote. (It gained above five percent in only five Northern states: Michigan, Vermont, New Hampshire, Massachusetts, and Maine.) Worse yet for Mahan's mood, Americans in 1844 elected Democrat slave owner James K. Polk as the next President of the United States.

The biggest depressor though for Mahan may have come out of his fourth trial, which occurred December 1843 at Federal Circuit Court in Ohio. Legally, Mahan himself wasn't involved directly, but his main benefactor William Dunlap certainly was, the man who had bailed Mahan out of a Kentucky prison in 1838. Mahan could not believe this long nightmare was dragging on after six long years. This trial wasn't for Mahan's criminal case, for which he was acquitted, but a follow-up to Greathouse's civil suit regarding Greathouse being compensated for the two enslaved blacks. Judge John McLean, Circuit Court Justice, summarized below how this issue came about in the first place between Greathouse and Dunlap before deciding the case. Legally, this was *Greathouse v. Dunlap*.

> OPINION OF THE COURT. This action of covenant is founded on the following instrument: Whereas, there is now depending in the Mason circuit court, in the state of

Kentucky, an action at common law, in which William Greathouse is plaintiff and John B. Mahan is defendant in which the said Mahan has been and is confined in the jail of Mason county for want of special bail; and it is agreed by the said William Greathouse to discharge him from custody on condition that William Dunlap, of Brown County, in the state of Ohio, shall enter into this bond: Now, therefore, I, the said William Dunlap, do by these presents bind and oblige myself, my heirs, &c that in case the said William Greathouse shall finally succeed in the said suit against the said John B. Mahan, that I, the said William Dunlap, will pay the amount of the recovery so finally had in the said suit against him the said Mahan, including all legal costs, dated the 22d of November, 1838." In each count it is averred, that on this bond being given Mahan was released from his imprisonment, and that in the case then pending there was recovered against Mahan the sum of sixteen hundred dollars in damages.

Dunlap made a "special plea" to the above agreement between he and Greathouse, namely that the bond had been "obtained by the fraud of Greathouse" and that he had "falsely and fraudulently procured a bill of indictment to be found a true bill by the grand jury," charging Mahan with aiding and assisting the escape of the slave, John.

Dunlap said Greathouse had made an oath before a Kentucky justice of the peace on August 22, 1838, stating a number of obvious falsehoods. For example, despite what Greathouse claimed to the justice of the peace, Mahan could not have been guilty of any indictment charges, was not a fugitive from Kentucky justice, had not been in Kentucky to commit any alleged crimes, and his extradition to Kentucky had been procured by Greathouse's "false and fraudulent misrepresentations" in order to lure Mahan to Mason County and there to induce Mahan's Ohio friends (who ended up being Dunlap, in part) to become financially responsible for Greathouse losing his slaves.

It was Dunlap's hope the judge would after-the-fact void the "contract" Dunlap entered into with Greathouse on November 22, 1838, in Maysville, solely because of Greathouse having set up the whole fraud.

Apparently, Dunlap, in 1843, was delinquent on taxes for some Ripley property and may have been in financial trouble himself.

The judge wrote in his ruling: "A judgment against Mahan was recovered, and the question is, whether the defendant can go behind that judgment." In other words, could Dunlap get his money back after already settling the contract?

Judge McClean ultimately decided that although what Dunlap presented was true, it wasn't enough to challenge the decided legal action. Greathouse won again. Technically, Mahan had been right. Greathouse would not be getting "25 cents" off him. He would be getting everything off Dunlap.

Oddly enough, Thomas L. Hamer represented Dunlap in *Greathouse vs. Dunlap*, perhaps to publicly wash himself of the stain of having refused Mahan a writ of habeas corpus. Or maybe Hamer was trying to rescue his own political future. None of it mattered to his political future though because Hamer would be dead within two years. He volunteered for the Mexican-American War, ended up a brigadier general, and died unexpectedly in Mexico.

Between the stress of having four trials, tuberculosis, losing daughter Mary Jane Mahan, financially owing a great deal of money, being an abolitionist and having to live under the Ohio Fugitive Slave Law of 1839 (at least until 1843), and the strains of day-to-day living, John B. Mahan began succumbing to all the weight.

In his last days, weakened by tuberculosis, he nonetheless felt warmed and strengthened by the continual presence of his wife and family, and that of his friends who stopped in to greet and pray, including Josiah Moore, the Pettijohns, Jacob Cumberland, Dr. Isaac Beck, and Rev. John Rankin, who was filling in as temporary pulpit supply for White Oak Presbyterian in Sardinia. He realized this was probably the end of his life—and yet also the beginning. He hoped to hear the words of Jesus, "Well done, good and faithful servant." He very much worried about the financial future of his wife and family, who had nearly nothing.

John Bennington Mahan died December 15, 1844, at age 43, at his Sardinia, Ohio, home. It was just ten days before Christmas, which normally would have been a happy time for his family.

Before making the decision to move her family closer to relatives in Illinois, Polly Mahan asked several newspapers to publish a copy of her husband's will, which had been drawn up years before when Mahan occupied a Maysville jail.

> Washington Prison, Kentucky, September 26, 1841
> In the name of God, Amen!
> I, John B. Mahan, Minister of the gospel of Jesus Christ, our Lord and Savior, being now in the 38th year of my age, in prison for the Testimony of the Gospel, and having the fear of God before my eyes, and also a humble hope that I shall attain the first resurrection, do now, in view of the frailty of human life, and the dangers to which my peculiar condition exposes me, make and

declare the following to be my last will and testament:

1st. Concerning myself—Lord, not my will, but thine be done.

2d. Concerning my beloved wife, Mary Mahan, and my three dear daughters, Mary Jane, Martha Ann, and Ann Eliza, and my four sons, dearly beloved, John Wesley, Isaac Sanders, Russel Bigelow, and Alexander Wickliffe, all these being the gift of God to me, I do give them up, and earnestly commend them to the providence and grace of Almighty God, and as instruments in the hands of God to them for good, I do in all confidence place them under the care of my good friends and the Chillicothe Presbytery, that my beloved wife, in her affliction and bereavement, may be comforted and sustained; that my dear daughters, being deprived of a father so early, may be instructed and provided for; and that my sons, much beloved, under the guidance, control and patronage of the said Chillicothe Presbytery, may be educated for the ministry.

3d. Concerning sectarianism, I will it all to the mo[l]es and bats, supposing it all to be the work of the devil to divide the children of the kingdom; for I regard the man as my brother in Christ (whatever his minor sentiments may be) who, worshipping in the fear of God, cherishes in his bosom a sacred regard for the rights of every member of the human family, and acts in strict conformity therewith; such person, having faith in the Redeemer, I regard as father, mother, or brother.

4th. Concerning my friends, to whom I have an alliance stronger than death, the Lord reward them according as their kindness to me has been.

5th. Concerning my enemies—which are many and hate me with a cruel hatred, and speak evil of me falsely for the sake of Christ and the Gospel—"the Lord forgive them, for they know not what they do."

6th. Now concerning the things for which I stand indicted here, I do affirm, before an omniscient God, that I am entirely unqualifiedly innocent. That for more than nineteen years I have not been in this county (Mason) either by myself or agent, on any business, at any time, either civil or criminal, lawful or unlawful; and further, that I have not sent any paper or document, written or printed, to any person or papers of this county, nor received any such paper or document from any such person or persons, or had any correspondence with any person or persons resident in this country, touching any such things as are charged against me in such indictment. For all of which things, I hold myself responsible to God at the great day of judgment. Signed and sealed, the year and day above written. John B. Mahan.

Of course, some newspapers around the nation printed news about his unexpected death, but not nearly as many as had reported about his legal trials. The *National Anti-Slavery Standard* wrote: "John B. Mahan—This tried friend of the Anti-Slavery cause, died recently, in Ohio. It would be recollected that he was imprisoned in 1838, for several weeks, in Kentucky, for aiding fugitives to escape. He was, however, acquitted on his trial, on the ground that the Kentucky courts had no right to sit in judgment on acts committed in Ohio."

Mahan left behind his loving wife Polly, and children Martha, Ann, John Wesley, Isaac, Russel, and Alexander. They were nearly penniless at his death. The Mahans would begin a new life in Illinois without the man they loved. You could say not just John B., but all the Mahans were victims to the Slave Power.

MAHAN'S "EULOGY": FROM THE PEOPLE WHO LOVED HIM
CHAPTER TWELVE

Nearly two months after Mahan's death, in February 1845, the *Cincinnati Morning Herald* printed a several-column-long article recapping what Mahan had gone through over the prior six to seven years. It included accurate information about his earlier trials, rehashed details for new readers, and helped the old remember. More than half of that very long article has appeared already in this work. In addition to what you have already read, the article set forth the belief that Mahan's trial had been a set up from the very beginning, and that Kentucky slaveowners had been out to make an example of Mahan. He truly was a martyr for his cause.

The article offered quite a tribute to Mahan and his character. It was also a desperate financial plea for Cincinnati readers to help the Mahan family.

A committee of six abolitionists formed after John B. Mahan's death in order to provide for his family. The group included close Sardinia friend Josiah Moore. They sent the below article to the *Cincinnati Morning Herald*. They were simply trying to memorialize and help out an old friend who had given up his life for the cause of abolition and his Lord.

> Mr. Mahan was compelled to sacrifice a large amount over and above the amount received from anti-slavery men, of his own, in defraying the expenses of the suit. Mr. Mahan's family, consisting of a widow and seven children, most of whom are small and unable to help themselves, are left without any means of support. If he

had been spared to remain with them, he would have, by his industry and economy, made a comfortable living for them, and perhaps the necessity for relief by the public would never have been made.

Gentle reader, you have now the facts of that unfortunate man and his now distressed family before you, and it is for you to determine what is your duty.

Resolved, That the object that the slaveholder citizens of Kentucky, in procuring the person of Mr. Mahan, had, was not to gratify a personal malice they had against him, but to make an example of him for the purpose of breaking down and destroying the feeling and principle of human rights, and deterring others by his punishment.

Resolved, That we deeply mourn the loss that community has sustained in being deprived of one of her brightest ornaments, and that the name and efforts of that high minded and benevolent man will be held in fond recollection by countless numbers of the down trodden and oppressed slaves, when those of his adversaries are lost in the vortex of forgetfulness, and that his unceasing perseverance in the cause of justice and human liberty will, to the latest time, be appreciated so long as there is a spark of virtue in the human heart.

Resolved, That the friends of justice and the salve are morally bound to restore to the bereaved and helpless family of that distinguished, independent and worthy citizen and philanthropist, all that he has been legally compelled to sacrifice in the great cause of justice and human rights.

Resolved, That while we appreciate the benevolence of Mr. Dunlap in offering to convey back the property deeded to him by Mr. Mahan for $950, we are of opinion that the amount of money necessary to redeem the property could be more beneficially appropriated in some other way, for the following reasons:

1—The property, though of value to some who could use it to the best advantage, will be of little value to the family of the deceased, because they have not the means nor are they in circumstances to use the property to advantage.

2—Owing to the present pressure of the times, the widow and helpless family, unaccustomed to making sales of property, might not for a long time, be able to effect a sale of it for near its value, and they are not able to wait, their circumstances require immediate relief.

Resolved, That we appoint a committee of six persons, into whose hands all monies collected shall be paid, and who shall appropriate the same as they may think most beneficially for the family, and that this committee consist of the following persons—James Gilliland, of Red Oak; Samuel G. Moore, of Russellville; Josiah Moore of Sardinia; Lewis Miller of Felicity; John R. Strain of Petersburgh, and Christian Donaldson of Cincinnati. Resolved, That Daniel Gilmer, Josiah Moore, and E.P. Evans, be appointed to publish an address to the public in behalf of the bereaved family of the late John B. Mahan.

Resolved, That the Rev. D. Gilmer be appointed agent to present the case of the family of the late J.B. Mahan, and solicit and receive funds in the bounds of the Chillicothe Presbytery.

Resolved, That the Secretary forward the proceedings of the meeting to the editor of the *Herald* and *Philanthropist* and request "The Watchman of the Valley" to copy— Josiah Moore, Secretary.

TO THE ANTI-SLAVERY FRIENDS OF OHIO

We would present to your consideration, the condition of the family of our much esteemed and lamented friend, the late J.B. Mahan—They are left without any means of support save a little personal property. A short time before his death his real estate was deed away to satisfy the unjust claims of Mr. Greathouse, of Kentucky. Mr. Mahan was not selected as the victim of the criminal and civil suits because the citizens of Kentucky had any particular hatred against him, but because they hoped through him to deter and punish the abolitionists in general. It was said to him in prison, that it was a pity that so fine a looking fellow should have to suffer, but that someone must be made an example of. Being prominent as an abolitionist, and having in possession considerable property, he was selected as the victim of slaveholding oppression. Through him they therefore struck the blow at the mass of the friends of the slave. And through him they reached them. The friends of oppression thought that if they could wound one of the members of the body, they could wound the body. We appeal to the body, to meet this assault upon one of its members, and so far as possible save it from suffering. Honesty calls upon Abolitionists to relieve this family as far as possible from the oppression of that assault.

Honor calls—Humanity calls. We might, sometimes ago, have called upon you to relieve Mr. M., who was in the power of the slaveholder, as far as you could; but we cannot now make this appeal; God has relieved hm. His cruel and relentless oppressors cannot reach him anymore. God has hid him in the grave, and will keep him secret until *their* wrath be past. But his destitute and helpless family are with us; and feel keenly the smart of oppression, and ask us for relief.

We would not, I am sure, have left Mr. M. had he lived, to struggle alone with the oppressor; we would have run to his relief. Then surely, we will not see his disconsolate widow and helpless and orphan children struggle with the oppressor, and pine away under his power. It is impossible for the friends of the slave every to remunerate the family for their losses in the affair of imprisonment and the consequent civil suit. The anguish which Mr. Mahan endured in the prison, shut up as he was in a filthy cell, in irons, can find no equivalent in gold or silver. He was separated from his family whom he dearly loved, for whose temporal and spiritual welfare he had the greatest possible anxiety. He was also in suspense concerning the result of his trial, knowing that testimony had ben suborned, and suspecting it would be again. He believed and hoped that he would not have to drag out a tedious imprisonment, but doubt, all the time, hung over the matter.

The following extract of (Mahan's) letter to a friend, while (Mahan was) in prison, will give some faint idea of his sufferings and his state of mind.—

"It is not small thing, indeed, to be severed from a beloved family to whom I am endeared by ties indissoluble;' to be carried out of my native State—torn from the society of thousands of friends, amongst whom and with whom I have spent years of happiness and months of joy; to be hurried into a prison in a foreign State, for no crime, and loaded with irons like a felon, where I can see no joyful sun, breathe no unfettered salubrious atmosphere, see no pleasing, shining countenance of heavenly messenger in human form, is no very pleasant thing, sir, I assure you. But there is hope at the bottom of this cup. I shall become again a locomotive being.

But if my fairest hopes should be blighted—if a gloomy prison is to be my lot—if I can see no more the living joy bespangled countenances of my wife and children dearer; of Christian friends—if I can taste no more the joys of social life, the sweets of liberty, "heaven's boon to all," I am resigned. No nerve shall quiver, nor knees like

Belshazzar's smite, no countenance of gloom, no tear of bitterness, no feeling of remorse; but all my words, when added up, shall be, "Heaven's will be done." What it may be asked, is the nearest equivalent that can be rendered for this suffering?

We answer, provide a comfortable home for his destitute and bereaved family; for whom he labored so hard to provide one. We will not certainly live in luxury and comfort, while they suffer for the common necessaries of life. While the slave holder assails us as a body for aiding the fugitive from oppression to a land of liberty, by pouncing on one who was in the foremost file, we will not surely leave his helpless wife and children to the mercy of the oppressor. We will run to their relief."

That father has gone to the grave—robbed by the oppressor of everything necessary to rear his dear children, and robbed, too, for doing what *we do* every opportunity afforded us. If only one or two had been doing that which awakened the ire of the oppressors, then had they not exposed themselves to the scorn of mankind, and disgraced their courts of justice to glut their vengeance on him; but because we helped their fugitives on our own soil to a land of freedom, they took vengeance on Mr. Mahan. You will see by the statement and resolutions accompanying this address, that a committee is appointed to received funds and appropriate them for the benefit of the family. Who will come to their relief? Who?

DANIEL GILMER, E.P. EVANS, JOSIAH MOORE.

Fully two years after Mahan's death, and after the above plea from close friends, *The Sandusky Clarion* (Ohio) reported sixty-three citizens of Clarksville (western Clinton County, thirty-five miles north of Sardinia) were still requesting the Ohio House of Representatives to remunerate the "widow and heirs of John Mahan, for losses sustained in consequence of his being delivered to the authorities of Kentucky by the executive of Ohio." Thirty-one other Ohioans joined in the Clarksville request. A similar request had occurred seven years earlier.

Many people loved him, including many fugitives who had been unable to thank him after having reached Canada. But they would always remember him.

What We Don't Know
CHAPTER THIRTEEN

It has been written that John Bennington Mahan was a Methodist local preacher and one day switched to being an ordained Presbyterian, probably around 1840. This was possible, but not probable for a number of reasons.

First, and probably foremost, Dr. Isaac Beck never referred to Mahan as a Presbyterian, or as a Presbyterian pastor, or as having switched to being a Presbyterian church member, but only always as a "Methodist local preacher," a term defined earlier. Beck even underlined the words "Methodist local preacher" in his 1892 letter. Dr. Beck knew John B. Mahan well as anyone, and certainly would have noted a denominational shift from one of his best friends, just as he had noted his own denominational shifts in his own recollections.

U.S. Presbyterians split in 1837-38, in small measure because of abolition, dividing into Old School and New School Presbyterians. Rankin chose the New School, which tended to be more evangelistic, not as adhered to strict doctrinal standards, and more supportive of abolition.

It would seem White Oak Presbyterian (Sardinia) chose the New School, too. For example, Rev. John Rankin himself was listed as a temporary pastor at Sardinia in 1844-45, about the time Mahan died. (The prior pastor Daniel Gilmer (New School) left on November 3, 1844.) Mahan may have attended White Oak Presbyterian to hear his old friend preach at some point before dying. Given Rankin was a temporary pastor, it could be assumed he visited Mahan during his final sickness and may have been present when

Mahan died. When John Rankin left Sardinia in 1845, the church had 126 members. John's son Rev. Samuel Rankin took over for his father in 1846 in Sardinia.

This author could not find any record anywhere of Mahan officially listed as a Presbyterian pastor, church officer or church member.

In addition, the Old School Chillicothe Presbytery records covering 1830-1845 do not mention anything at all about any John B. Mahan, not even his name. Also, a pastoral switch from Methodist to Presbyterian for Mahan was unlikely for a number of reasons, but the greatest would have been doctrinal differences.

That said, Mahan, again, before his 1844 death, could have stopped working at his Methodist Church to worship at White Oak Presbyterian given his health and the presence of Rankin. A possible change in worship locations would have made some sense given at least one witness against Mahan at two of his trials had the surname of Hamilton—a surname long-associated with the Slab Camp Methodists. Mahan, of course, as a Methodist local preacher, would have known the family well. It would make sense if he chose not to worship as a Methodist, that is, if Hamilton had been a Methodist and was attending.

Beck was Disciples of Christ. Mahan could have gone there to worship with him. But if anything, given his Baptist upbringing, it would have made more sense for Mahan to worship with the Baptists, who had a Sardinia church beginning about 1840 that lasted several years, and whose founder, Rev. Hampton Pangburn, was an abolitionist.

So if Mahan was never a Presbyterian pastor, or even Presbyterian, and an Old School Presbyterian Church did not exist in Sardinia or anywhere near Sardinia, how do we explain Mahan, in his last will and testament writing these words regarding his children: "I do in all confidence place them under the care of my good friends and the Chillicothe Presbytery [ed. note, Old School], that my beloved wife, in her affliction and bereavement, may be comforted and sustained; that my dear daughters, being deprived of a father so early, may be instructed and provided for; and that my sons, much beloved, under the guidance, control and patronage of the said Chillicothe Presbytery, may be educated for the ministry."

Of the six men heading up the committee to raise money for Mahan's family, i.e., James Gilliland, Samuel G. Moore; Josiah Moore, Daniel Gilmer, John R. Strain, and Christian Donaldson, the author could positively identify only one person with then-current Chillicothe Presbytery ties: Strain.

Rev. Daniel Gilmer in 1841 left the Chillicothe Presbytery for the Presbytery in Ripley (New School), James Gilliland did the same in 1838, Samuel G. Moore attended a New School church in Russellville, and so did Josiah Moore in Sardinia. Christian Donaldson was a Cincinnati hardware store owner and had been on the Ohio Anti-Slavery Society executive committee. Only John R. Strain could be directly tied to an Old School church in 1844.

On a sad note, Christian Donaldson became a member of the Mahan committee even though his only daughter had passed away at age twenty just eighteen days after Mahan. This speaks volumes about his character, and also of his compassion for Mahan's family.

That said, it is possible Chillicothe Presbytery, out of goodwill, concern for Mahan, and the cause of abolition, before his first or third trials—even though he was not Old School Presbyterian—unofficially promised to care for his family should Mahan die young. If he had been associated with a local Presbyterian church, the request most assuredly would have gone to the local church. Having the Old School presbytery involved years prior was not out of the realm of possibilities. Mahan may have simply been following through on an old promise made by the Chillicothe Presbytery. But again, this is mere speculation, too.

NOTES

AUTHOR'S INTRODUCTION

9 *"John B. Mahan, a tall"*: Birney, William. *James G. Birney and His Times: the genesis of the republican party with some account of abolition movements in the south before 1828*. New York: D. Appleton and Company, 1890, 167.
10 *"The year 1820"*; Grim, Paul R. *The Rev. John Rankin, Early Abolitionist*. Ohio Archaeological and Historical Quarterly, Volume 46, 222.
10 *"He wrote Letters"*: Ibid., 227.
10 *"He co-founded the Ohio"*: Ibid., 229.
11 *"Harriet Beecher Stowe's"*: Ibid., 241.
11 *"So you're the little"*: Vollaro, Daniel R. *Lincoln, Stowe, and the "Little Woman/Great War" Story: The Making, and Breaking, of a Great American Anecdote*. Journal of the Abraham Lincoln Association, 2009, Volume 30, 18.
11 *"Mahan also played"*: Ohio Anti-Slavery Convention. *Proceedings of the Ohio Anti-Slavery Convention. Held at Putnam, on the twenty-second, twenty-third, and twenty-fourth of April, 1835*. Putnam, 1835, 1.
11 *"In the early years"*: Grim, Paul R. *The Rev. John Rankin, Early Abolitionist*. Ohio Archaeological and Historical Quarterly, Volume 46, 228. (Courtesy of Ohio History Connection.)
11 *"...had pricey bounties"*: Ibid., 237.
12 *"...decided the outcome of the 1838"*: *Flemingsburg Kentuckian*, October 12, 1838, 2.
13 *"...actually snuffed out any and all"*: Stephens, Alexander H. *A Compendium of the History of the United States from the Earliest Settlements to 1872*. American Foundation Publication, Bridgewater, Va. 1999, 363.
13 *"Fugitive Slave Law"*: Preston, Emmett D. *The Fugitive Slave Acts in Ohio*. The Journal of Negro History, Volume 28 (4), 427.
13 *"The Ohio House also in early 1839"*: *Daily Herald and Gazette* (Cleveland, Ohio), January 19, 1839, 2.
14 *"...a Methodist 'local preacher'"*: Dr. Isaac M. Beck letter to Wilbur H. Siebert, December 26, 1892. (Courtesy of Ohio History Connection.)
14 *"...he wrote his wife"*: *The Philanthropist* (Cincinnati, Ohio), October 23, 1838, 4.
14 *"He also spoke truth"*: *The Western Citizen*, November 9, 1838, 1.

CHAPTER 1

18 *"...due to opposing slavery:"* Rivington, Kate. *In its Midst: An Analysis of One Hundred Southern-Born Anti-Slavery Activists.* Australasian Journal of American Studies, Volume 38 (1), 45-78.
18 *"...were developing the logistics":* Siebert, Wilbur H. *Beginnings of the Underground Railroad in Ohio.* Ohio Archaeological and Historical Quarterly, Volume 56 (1), 70-93. (Courtesy of Ohio History Connection.)
18 *"Some supported the American":* Debate at the Lane Seminary, Cincinnati, Speech of James A. Thome, of Kentucky, at the Annual Meeting of the American Anti-Slavery Society, May 6, 1834. Letter of the Rev. Dr. Samuel H. Cox, Against the American Colonization Society. Boston, Garrison & Knapp, 1834.
19 *"Other Ohioans tried catching…":* Hand, Greg. *Cincinnati Magazine.* February 18, 2016.
19 *"Slave Act of 1793":* New York State Parks publication. https://parks.ny.gov › documents › historic-preservation › FugitiveSlaveAct1793.pdf. Retrieved July 1, 2025.
20 *"Ohio Constitutional Convention":* McCullough, David. *The Pioneers: The Heroic Story of the Settlers Who Brought the American Ideal West.* New York, Simon & Schuster, 2019, 144-146.
20 *"...had to be carried in":* Ibid., 145.
20 *"...enact very strict laws":* Bill of Rights Institute. Ohio State Constitution, 1803 and Black Code, 1804. https://billofrightsinstitute.org/activities/ohio-state-constitution-1803-and-black-code-1804. Retrieved July 1, 2025.
21 *"The 1807 Act, Section 1":* Ibid.
22 *"...in Kentucky, for example":* Mission US. Kentucky Slave Codes (1794-1850). https://www.mission-us.org/teach/flight-to-freedom/resources/kentucky-slave-codes-1794-1850/ Retrieved July 1, 2025.
22 *"Kentucky Slave Stealing Statute":* Hodges, Albert G. *A Digest of the Statute Laws of Kentucky.* Frankfort, 1834, 1302-03.
22 *"That if any person":* Ibid.
23 *"The possibility of being sold":* Salafia, Matthew. *Searching for Slavery: Fugitive Slaves in the Ohio River Valley Borderland, 1830–1860.* Ohio Valley History, Volume 8(4), 38-63.
23 *"1840 U.S. Census":* 1840 Census: Compendium of the Enumeration of the Inhabitants and Statistics of the United States.

https://www2.census.gov/library/publications/decennial /1840/1840v3/1840c-05.pdf Retrieved July 18, 2025.
24 *"It initiated printing in"*: *Greene County Gazette*, March 31, 1836, 3.
"Southern-minded Cincinnati": *The Cleveland Herald*, December 9, 1835, 3.
24 *"The entire sequence of events"*: *Carroll Free Press*, August 26, 1836, 1.
25 *"The doctrines of the Abolitionists"*: *The History of Brown County Ohio*. Chicago, W.H. Beers & Co., 1883, 314.
25 *"...massive eighteen-foot-wide"*: Birney, William. *James G. Birney and His Times: the genesis of the republican party with some account of abolition movements in the south before 1828*. New York: D. Appleton and Company, 1890, 218.
25 *"The maelstrom started"*: *Carroll Free Press*, August 26, 1836, 1.
26 *"Morgan Neville"*: Morgan Neville letter to Thomas Jefferson, December 10, 1819. National Archives, Founders Online. https://founders.archives.gov/documents/Jefferson/03-15-02-0246 Retrieved July 1, 2025.
26 *"Noted the Carroll Free Press"*: *Carroll Free Press*, August 26, 1836, 1.
27 *"Publishing this on Monday"*: Ibid.
29 *"From the Carroll Free Press"*: Ibid.
31 *"Davies actually participated"*: Birney, William. *James G. Birney and His Times: the genesis of the republican party with some account of abolition movements in the south before 1828*. New York: D. Appleton and Company, 1890, 247.

CHAPTER 2

33 *"The first white settler"*: Wardlaw, Joseph G. *Genealogy of the Wardlaw Family: with some account of other families with which it is connected*. York, South Carolina, 1929, 181.
33 *"He was a Presbyterian"*: Ibid., 182.
33 *"The first Presbyterian church"*: Thompson, Carl N. *Historical Collections of Brown County*, Hammer Graphics, Piqua (Ohio), 1969, 1024.
33 *"...a number of Methodist families"*: Ibid., 1069.
33 *"History of Brown County"*: *The History of Brown County Ohio*. Chicago, W.H. Beers & Co., 1883, 674.
34 *"Jacob volunteered as a missionary"*: Wilmore, Rev. August Cleland. *History of the White River Conference of the United Brethren in Christ*. Church of the United Brethren in Christ United Brethren Publishing House, Dayton, 1925, 35-36.

34 *"United Brethren in Christ historian"*: Ibid.
35 *"Mahan settled in Perry Township"*: *The History of Brown County, Ohio*. Chicago, W. H. Beers and Company, 1883. Page 481.
35 *"Mahan married Polly"*: Ohio, County Marriages, 1789-2016", *FamilySearch* https://www.familysearch.org/ark:/ 61903/1:1:XZ86-DVD : Sat Mar 09 04:36:59 UTC 2024), Entry for John B. Mahan and Polly Stairs, 1820.
35 *"...school teacher"*: Thompson, Carl N. *Historical Collections of Brown County*, Hammer Graphics, Piqua (Ohio), 1969, 756.
35 *"...township fence viewer"*: *The History of Brown County, Ohio*. Chicago, W.H. Beers & Company, 1883, 670.
35 *"...overseer of the poor"*: Ibid.
36 *"He and John Dunham built"*: Ibid., 678.
36 *"Temperance Tavern"*: Thompson, Carl N. *Historical Collections of Brown County*, Hammer Graphics, Piqua (Ohio), 1969, 182.
36 *"According to Dr. Isaac Beck"*: Dr. Isaac M. Beck letter to Wilbur H. Siebert, December 26, 1892. (Courtesy of Ohio History Connection.)
37 *"The first two homes built in Sardinia"*: Thompson, Carl N. *Historical Collections of Brown County*, Hammer Graphics, Piqua (Ohio), 1969, 182.
37 *"...given authority by his denomination"*: Parker, Edmond Thomas. *The Methodist Circuit Rider in the Old Northwest*, 1966, Master's thesis.
38 *"...a Methodist local preacher"*: Dr. Isaac M. Beck letter to Wilbur H. Siebert, December 26, 1892. (Courtesy of Ohio History Connection.) https://ecommons.luc.edu/ luc_theses/2186 Retrieved July 1, 2025.
38 *"He did not self-identify"*: Ohio Anti-Slavery Convention. *Proceedings of the Ohio Anti-Slavery Convention. Held at Putnam, on the twenty-second, twenty-third, and twenty-fourth of April, 1835*. Putnam, 1835, 1.
38 *"A number of early Methodist families"*: *The History of Brown County, Ohio*. Chicago, W. H. Beers and Company, 1883. Page 668.
38 *"Erastus Mahan, John's nephew"*: Mahan, Erastus. *Friends of Liberty on the Mackinaw*. McClean County (Ill.) Historical Society, Bloomington. Volume 1, 1899, 397-399. https://archive.org/details/transactionsof mc01mcle/page/n901/mode/2up?q=Mahan. Retrieved July 1, 2025.
39 *"Dr. Beck delivered"*: Dr. Isaac M. Beck letter to Wilbur H. Siebert, December 26, 1892. (Courtesy of Ohio History Connection.)
39 *"The Troy (Ohio) Times read"*: *The Troy Times*, June 26, 1839, 2.
40 *"Samuel Gist, a wealthy English landowner"*: Powell, C. A., Kavanaugh, B. T., and Christy, D. *Transplanting Free Negroes to Ohio from 1815 to 1858*.

The Journal of Negro History, 1916, 1(3), 302–17. https://doi.org/10.2307/3035625. Retrieved July 1, 2025.
41 *"...the reticent Virginia executrix:"* McGroarty, William Buckner. *Exploration in Mass Emancipation.* The William and Mary College Quarterly Historical Magazine, Volume 21(3), 209.
41 *"Gist's free blacks inherited":* Ibid., 213.
41 *"...inked the deal":* Ibid., 219.
42 *"The Gist settlers eventually would become embroiled:"* Ibid., 220.
42 *"Notwithstanding this, we find":* Ohio Anti-Slavery Convention. *Proceedings of the Ohio Anti-Slavery Convention.* Held at Putnam, on the twenty-second, twenty-third, and twenty-fourth of April, 1835, 17.
43 *"Eliza Jane Johnson":* The Clermont Courier, March 17, 1838, 3.
43 *"...by their "free" papers":* Coleman, J. Winston Jr. *Slavery Times in Kentucky.* Chapel Hill, N.C. The University of North Carolina press, 1940, 205.
43 *"...though Johnson's supposed slave owner":* The Liberator, April 20, 1838, 4.
43 *"James Huggins":* The Liberty Hall and Cincinnati Gazette, March 8, 1838, 4.
44 *"...war ought to be immediately":* Ibid., 127.
44 *"It literally took an act":* Cochran, William, C. *The Western Reserve and the Fugitive Slave Law.* Cleveland. The Western Reserve Historical Society, Publication No. 101, 1920, 74-75.
45 *"Former U.S. President John Quincy Adams":* Stephens, Alexander H. *A Compendium of the History of the United States from the Earliest Settlements to 1872.* American Foundation Publication, Bridgewater, Va. 1999, 359.
45 *"Lane Seminary (Presbyterian)":* Debate at the Lane Seminary, Cincinnati, Speech of James A. Thome, of Kentucky, at the Annual Meeting of the American Anti-Slavery Society, May 6, 1834. Letter of the Rev. Dr. Samuel H. Cox, Against the American Colonization Society. Boston, Garrison & Knapp, 1834.
45 *"...entertained but two questions":* Ibid., 3.
46 *"James Bradley...addressed us":* Ibid., 4.
47 *"...Mahan, joined to inaugurate...":* Ohio Anti-Slavery Convention. *Proceedings of the Ohio Anti-Slavery Convention. Held at Putnam, on the twenty-second, twenty-third, and twenty-fourth of April, 1835.* Putnam, 1835, 1.
47 *"Six Brown Countians":* Ibid.
47 *"We believe slavery to be a sin":* Ibid., 5-8.

50 *"...committee to nominate officers"*: Ibid., 3.
50 *"...seven-man "resolutions" committee"*: Ibid., 4.
50 *"The resolutions committee adopted"*: Ibid., 4-5.
51 *"Mahan was named "Manager"*: Ibid., 41.
51 *"Protesters attacked Rankin"*: Grim, Paul R. *The Rev. John Rankin, Early Abolitionist*. Ohio Archaeological and Historical Quarterly, Volume 46, 230-31. (Courtesy of Ohio History Connection.)
52 *"...million pieces of anti-slavery literature"*: Wyatt-Brown, Bertram. The Abolitionists' Postal Campaign of 1835. The Journal of Negro History Volume 50(4), 227-238.
52 *"...nationwide nearly tripled"*: Ibid., 237.
52 *"Rankin had taken six months off"*: Grim, Paul R. *The Rev. John Rankin, Early Abolitionist*. Ohio Archaeological and Historical Quarterly, Volume 46, 231. (Courtesy of Ohio History Connection.)

CHAPTER 3

54 *"We do know things about Josiah"*: The History of Brown County, Ohio. Chicago, W.H. Beers & Co., 1883, 290-91.
54 *"He was a temperance advocate:"* Ibid.
54 *"...a dozen Pettijohn families"*: The History of Brown County, Ohio. Chicago, W. H. Beers and Company, 1883. Page 666-67.
55 *"...much more about Beck"*: Isaac M. Beck letter to Wilbur H. Siebert, December 26, 1892. (Courtesy of Ohio History Connection.)
55 *"...his contributions to the Underground"*: The History of Brown County, Ohio. Chicago, W.H. Beers & Co., 1883, 284.
55 *"...not just because his maternal uncle"*: Isaac M. Beck letter to Wilbur H. Siebert, December 26, 1892. (Courtesy of Ohio History Connection.)
55 *"Beck's first job at age seventeen"*: The History of Brown County, Ohio. Chicago, W.H. Beers & Co., 1883, 284.
55 *"...he relocated to where the town of Sardinia"*: Isaac M. Beck letter to Wilbur H. Siebert, December 26, 1892. (Courtesy of Ohio History Connection.)
55 *"...a license to practice medicine"*: The History of Brown County, Ohio. Chicago, W.H. Beers & Co., 1883, 284.
55 *"It was Mahan who probably built Beck's home"*: Thompson, Carl N. *Historical Collection of Brown County*. Hammer Graphics, Piqua (Ohio), 1969, 36. The name mentioned as builder of Beck's home was John

Magan, most certainly a typographical error. It would make sense a saw mill operator also could work as a carpenter to build Beck's home.
55 *"Over time he would change political"*: Isaac M. Beck letter to Wilbur H. Siebert, December 26, 1892. (Courtesy of Ohio History Connection.)
56 *"Here are his own words"*: Ibid.
57 *"This group of abolitionist Presbyterian pastors"*: Galbraith, Rev. R.C. *The History of the Chillicothe Presbytery: From Its Organization in 1799 to 1889.* Chillicothe (Ohio), 1889, 146-47.
58 *"James Gilliland could be called the 'Grandfather'"*: Ibid., 144.
58 *"...a Boston abolitionist newspaper"*: *The Liberator*, January 1, 1831.
59 *"....could count on the support"*: Isaac M. Beck letter to Wilbur H. Siebert, December 26, 1892. (Courtesy of Ohio History Connection.)
59 *"...but it had rules"*: Ibid.
59 *"Possibly the Sardinian guiding more"*: Ibid.
60 *"...that Beck shared about real Sardinians"*: Ibid.

CHAPTER 4

68 *"An example of how editors"*: *Vermont State Journal*, May 31, 1836, 2.
70 *"Just Cincinnati alone..."*: Suess, Jeff. *Cincinnati has had 124 newspapers. Their digital archives make our history more complete.* Cincinnati Enquirer, April 20, 2025. https://www.cincinnati.com/story/news/2025/04/20/access-history-cincinnati-124-different-newspapers/83079848007/ Retrieved July 2, 2025.
70 *"...was Warren G. Harding"*: Russell, Thomas H. *The Illustrious Life and Work of Warren G. Harding, Twenty-Ninth President of the United States: From Farm to White House.* 1923, 56-58.

CHAPTER 5

72 *"Up to $2,500 in reward money"*: Grim, Paul R. *The Rev. John Rankin, Early Abolitionist.* Ohio Archaeological and Historical Quarterly, Volume 46, 237.
72 *"Here is the warrant"*: *The Liberator*, November 2, 1838, 2.
73 *"On September 6 issued his own warrant"*: *Maumee City Express*, December 15, 1838, 2.
74 *"...deputy Vince Crabb"*: Hagedorn, Ann. *Beyond the River: The Untold Story of the Heroes of the Underground Railroad.* New York, Simon & Schuster, 2002, 153-56.
75 *"...simply ignored the writ of habeas corpus"*: Ibid., 156.

75 *"That for the last six months"*: The Philanthropist, December 18, 1838, 1.
75 *"Lewis Pettijohn"*: Ibid.
76 *"The Philanthropist on October 23"*: The Philanthropist, October 23, 1838, 1.
76 *"On September 22"*: Ibid.
77 *"On September 26"*: Ibid.
78 *"...friend on October 1"*: Ibid.
79 *"On October 2"*: Ibid.
80 *"Polly soon visited her husband"*: Mahan, Erastus. *Friends of Liberty on the Mackinaw.* McClean County (Ill.) Historical Society, Bloomington. Volume 1, 1899, 436-441. https://archive.org/details/transactionsof mc01mcle/page/n901/mode/2up?q=Mahan. Retrieved July 1, 2025.
80 *"...he penned these letters..."*: The Philanthropist, October 23, 1838, 1.
81 *"The Cleveland Daily Herald and Gazette published letters"*: Daily Herald and Gazette, October 30, 1838, 2.
84 *"The Journal and Register"*: The Journal and Register, Washington, Mason County, Kentucky October 4, 1838.
86 *"Vance lost by a mere"*: Volpe, Vernon L. *The Ohio Election of 1838: Study in the Historical Method?.* https://resources.ohiohistory.org/ohj/search/display. php?page=46&searchterm =105th&vol=95&pages=85-100 Retrieved July 2, 2025. (Courtesy of Ohio History Connection.)
86 *"Vance also had hurt"*: Hur, Hyun. *Radical Antislavery and Personal Liberty Laws in Antebellum Ohio, 1803-1857.* PhD diss., doctoral dissertation, Univ. of Wisconsin, 2012, 87.
87 *"...he would be leaving Congress"*: Maumee City Express, June 2, 1838, 3.
87 *"...with Hamer literally announcing"*: (Cleveland) Daily Herald and Gazette, November 17, 1838, 2.
87 *"The Western Citizen"*: The Western Citizen, November 9, 1838, 1.
87 *"The Daily Herald and Gazette"*: Daily Herald and Gazette, October 30, 1838, 2.
88 *"Grant was attending school in Ripley"*: Grant, U.S. *Personal Memoirs of U.S. Grant.* Old Saybook (Conn.), Konecky & Konecky, 1885, 23.
88 *"...one of the ablest men Ohio"*: Ibid., 24.
88 *"There was probably no time"*: Ibid., 25.

CHAPTER 6

90 *"...John Chambers for $300"*: Isaac M. Beck letter to Wilbur H.

Siebert, December 26, 1892. (Courtesy of Ohio History Connection.)
90 *"Including Chambers, he had three"*: Reid, Joseph B. and Reeder, Henry R. *Trial of Rev. John B. Mahan, for felony: in the Mason Circuit Court of Kentucky: commencing on Tuesday, the 13th, and terminating on Monday the 19th of November, 1838.* Cincinnati, 1838, 8.
90 *"Illinois abolitionist Elijah Lovejoy"*: *The Liberator*, December 8, 1837, 1.
90 *"...had been born Southerners"*: Rivington, Kate. *In its Midst: An Analysis of One Hundred Southern-Born Anti-Slavery Activists.* Australasian Journal of American Studies, Volume 38(1), 45-78.
91 *"...this same Reid who owned slaves"*: Reid, Joseph B. and Reeder, Henry R. *Trial of Rev. John B. Mahan, for felony: in the Mason Circuit Court of Kentucky: commencing on Tuesday, the 13th, and terminating on Monday the 19th of November, 1838.* Cincinnati, 1838, 83.
91 *"...meandering from his script"*: Ibid., 3-8.
92 *"...his Maysville neighbors desired"*: Ibid.
95 *"...the kindness of Kentucky Governor Clark"*: *Flemingsburg Kentuckian*, October 12, 1838, 2.
96 *"I repeat that your duties"*: Reid, Joseph B. and Reeder, Henry R. *Trial of Rev. John B. Mahan, for felony: in the Mason Circuit Court of Kentucky: commencing on Tuesday, the 13th, and terminating on Monday the 19th of November, 1838.* Cincinnati, 1838, 6.
97 *"I have given you the law"*: Ibid., 8.
98 *"Mr. Huggins"*: *The Liberator*, October 12, 1838, 3.
102 *"...two additional prosecution witnesses"*: Reid, Joseph B. and Reeder, Henry R. *Trial of Rev. John B. Mahan, for felony: in the Mason Circuit Court of Kentucky: commencing on Tuesday, the 13th, and terminating on Monday the 19th of November, 1838.* Cincinnati, 1838, 9.
104 *"The letter dated August 4"*: Ibid., 10.
105 *"Hamilton family as Methodists"*: Thompson, Carl N. *Historical Collections of Brown County*, Hammer Graphics, Piqua (Ohio), 1969, 1069.
105 *"All reasonable expectation"*: Reid, Joseph B. and Reeder, Henry R. *Trial of Rev. John B. Mahan, for felony: in the Mason Circuit Court of Kentucky: commencing on Tuesday, the 13th, and terminating on Monday the 19th of November, 1838.* Cincinnati, 1838, 12.
106 *"Their names were David Henderson"*: Ibid., 12.
106 *"Judge Reid read the indictment"*: Ibid., 12.
108 *"...overheard a conversation in Sardinia"*: Ibid., 13.
111 *"Perrigo was called to the stand"*: Ibid., 15-20.

118 *"The Judge allowed a second reading"*: Ibid., 21.
119 *"An observer wrote about"*: Ibid., 21.
120 *"...that a citizen of Ohio"*: Ibid., 23.
120 *"I understand these facts to be in evidence"*: Ibid., 41.
121 *"Prosecution lawyer Payne maintained"*: Ibid., 62.
122 *"War between Kentucky and Ohio?"*: Ibid., 73.
123 *"Judge Reid opined his own"*: Ibid., 79.
124 *"...from the hometown Maysville Eagle"*: *Daily Herald and Gazette*, November 27, 1838, 2.
126 *"Sardinia Anti-Slavery Society"*: *The History of Brown County, Ohio*. Chicago, W.H. Beers & Co., 1883, 314-315.
127 *"Written by Mahan"*: Reid, Joseph B. and Reeder, Henry R. *Trial of Rev. John B. Mahan, for felony: in the Mason Circuit Court of Kentucky: commencing on Tuesday, the 13th, and terminating on Monday the 19th of November, 1838*. Cincinnati, 1838, 86-88.

CHAPTER 7

133 *"Lame Duck Governor Joseph Vance"*: *The Troy Times*, December 5, 1938, 1.
134 *"On December 8"*: (Cleveland) *Daily Herald and Gazette*, December 8, 1838, 3.
136 *"Charles Atherton of New Hampshire"*: Stephens, Alexander H. *A Compendium of the History of the United States from the Earliest Settlements to 1872*. American Foundation Publication, Bridgewater, Va. 1999, 361-363.
137 *"Morris went down fighting"*: *The Liberator*, February 15, 1839, 3.
137 *"Democrat Benjamin Tappan"*: *The Cleveland Herald*, March 20, 1839, 1.
138 *"The General Assembly of Ohio"*: *Daily Herald and Gazette*, January 19, 1839, 2.
138 *"Resolved, That in the opinion"*: Ibid.
139 *"State senator from Maysville"*: *Daily Herald and Gazette*, December 27, 1838, 2.
140 *"Ohio Governor Wilson Shannon presented"*: *Journal of the Senate of Ohio, as the First Session of the Thirty-Seventh General Assembly; Held in the City of Columbus, and Commencing Monday, December 3, 1838*. Columbus, 1838-39, 224.
140 *"Wade, an avid abolitionist"*: Ibid., 244-245.
141 *"An impatient Ohio House"*: Ibid., 248.

141 *"Isaiah Morris, a Whig"*: Ibid., 255.
142 *"...eighty-four Ripley women"*: Ibid., 300.
142 *"Sen. Benjamin Wade, of Northern Ohio"*: Ibid., 346.
143 *"Massachusetts Congressman John Quincy Adams"*: The Liberator, February 25, 1837, 4.
143 *"The Western Citizen"*: The Western Citizen, February 1, 1839, 3.
143 *"...Mahan's relief petition"*: Journal of the Senate of Ohio, as the First Session of the Thirty-Seventh General Assembly; Held in the City of Columbus, and Commencing Monday, December 3, 1838. Columbus, 1838-39, 334.
144 *"Senate and House overwhelmingly"*: Journal of the Senate of Ohio, as the First Session of the Thirty-Seventh General Assembly; Held in the City of Columbus, and Commencing Monday, December 3, 1838. Columbus, 1838-39, 393.
144 *"As expected, The Philanthropist"*: The Philanthropist, November 18, 1840.
144 *"Below contains the entire...."*: Galbreath, Charles B. *Ohio's Fugitive Slave Law [of 1839]*. Ohio Archaeological and Historical Quarterly, Volume 34, 216-40. Https://resources.ohiohistory.org/ohj/browse/display pages.php?display%5B%5D=0034&display%5B%5D=216&display%5B%5D=240 Retrieved July 2, 2025. (Courtesy of Ohio History Connection.)

CHAPTER 8

154 *"Mahan realized The Philanthropist"*: The Philanthropist, October 2, 1838, 6.
154 *"The Philanthropist on October 4"*: The Philanthropist, October 4, 1838, 1.
154 *"On Sunday April 7"*: Hagedorn, Ann. *Beyond the River: The Untold Story of the Heroes of the Underground Railroad*. New York, Simon & Schuster, 2002, 185.
155 *"A week later, again on a Sunday"*: Ibid., 186.
155 *"On Monday April 15, next morning"*: Ibid., 187.
155 *"On Sunday April 21"*: Ibid., 187-188.
156 *"Dr. Isaac Beck later wrote"*: Isaac M. Beck letter to Wilbur H. Siebert, December 26, 1892. (Courtesy of Ohio History Connection.)
157 *"John B. Mahan, an open-hearted"*: Vermont Telegraph, June 19, 1839, 2.
158 *"An August ad in the Rochester Freeman"*: The Rochester Freeman, August 14, 1839, 4.

159 *"Carberry claimed he was the victim"*: *Wilmington Democrat and Herald*, May 3, 1839, 2. (Republished from *Ohio Statesman* of April 13.)
160 *"But first, from The Liberator"*: *The Liberator*, November 22, 1839, 3.
162 *"The first negative press"*: *Wilmington Democrat and Herald*, May 3, 1839, 2. (Republished from *The Ohio Statesman*, April 13, 1839.)
163 *"Urbana Democrat and Herald"*: *Urbana Democrat and Herald*, October 25, 1839, 3.
164 *"Honesty is the best policy"*: (Cleveland) *Weekly Plain Dealer*, October 24, 1839, 3.
164 *"Cleveland Daily Herald"*: *Cleveland Daily Herald*, October 21, 1839, 2.
165 *"The Baltimore Sun"*: *The Baltimore Sun*, October 22, 1839, 1.

CHAPTER 9

166 *"Mahan personally in 1839-40"*: Hagedorn, Ann. *Beyond the River: The Untold Story of the Heroes of the Underground Railroad*. New York, Simon & Schuster, 2002, 190.
167 "The Cincinnati Enquirer on June 1": *The Cincinnati Enquirer*, June 1, 1841.
168 *"The Whole Case of John B. Mahan"*: *National Anti-Slavery Standard*, July 22, 1841, 1.

CHAPTER 10

177 *"According to Dr. Beck"*: Isaac M. Beck letter to Wilbur H. Siebert, December 26, 1892. (Courtesy of Ohio History Connection.)
177 *"…did his own leg work"*: Hagedorn, Ann. *Beyond the River: The Untold Story of the Heroes of the Underground Railroad*. New York, Simon & Schuster, 2002, 190.
178 *"To the friends of the slave in Ohio"*: *The Oberlin Evangelist*, August 4, 1841, 8.
180 *"Georgetown Democratic Standard"*: *Democratic Standard*, August 31, 1841, 3.
182 *"On September 17, 1841"*: *Clermont Courier*, September 25, 1841, 3.
183 *"In much of 1843"*: Hagedorn, Ann. *Beyond the River: The Untold Story of the Heroes of the Underground Railroad*. New York, Simon & Schuster, 2002, 226-228.
183 *"…would run for U.S. President"*: Birney, William. *James G. Birney and His Times: the genesis of the republican party with some account of abolition movements in the south before 1828*. New York: D. Appleton and Company,

1890, preface vi.
184 *"...for U.S. Vice President"*: Morris, B.F. *The Life of Thomas Morris: Pioneer and long a legislator of Ohio and U.S. Senator from 1833 to 1839.* Cincinnati: Moore, Wilstach, Keys & Overend, 1836, 307.
184 *"...to claim 'Black Bill'"*: Preston, Emmett D. *The Fugitive Slave Acts in Ohio.* The Journal of Negro History, Volume 28 (4), 438.
184 *"At trial in Marion on August 27"*: Ibid., 440.
185 *"...Virginians held Black Bill"*: Ibid., 442.
185 *"...repealed January 19, 1843"*: Cochran, William, C. *The Western Reserve and the Fugitive Slave Law.* Cleveland. The Western Reserve Historical Society, Publication No. 101, 1920, 77.

CHAPTER 11

186 *"Doctors did not understand until the 1880s"*: McCutcheon, Marc. *The Writer's Guide to Everyday Life in the 1800s.* Cincinnati, Writer's Digest Books, 1993, 160-161.
186 *"According to Mayo Clinic"*: Mayo Clinic online. https://www.mayoclinic.org/diseases-conditions/tuberculosis/symptoms-causes/syc-20351250 Retrieved July 3, 2025.
187 *"Adam Bender, an "insane" person"*: (Georgetown) Democratic Standard, August 3, 1841, 4.
187 *"It was Rush who believed"*: McCutcheon, Marc. *The Writer's Guide to Everyday Life in the 1800s.* Cincinnati, Writer's Digest Books, 1993, 161.
188 *"Mary Jane passing away"*: Hagedorn, Ann. *Beyond the River: The Untold Story of the Heroes of the Underground Railroad.* New York, Simon & Schuster, 2002, 228.
188 *"Or by the brutal whipping"*: National Anti-Slavery Standard, August 8, 1844, 1.
188 *"Greathouse vs. Dunlap"*: Greathouse v. Dunlap. Circuit Court District, Ohio. December term, 1843. Case No. 5,742. https://law.resource.org/ pub/us/case/reporter/F.Cas/0010.f.cas /0010.f.cas.1062.pdf Retrieved July 3, 2025.
189 *"...obtained by the fraud of Greathouse"*: Ibid.
189 *"...justice of the peace on August 22, 1838"*: Ibid.
190 *"...was delinquent on taxes"*: Democratic Standard, December 10, 1844, 4.
191 *"Polly Mahan asked several"*: The Liberator, April 11, 1845, 1.
193 *"The National Anti-Slavery Standard wrote"*: The National Anti-Slavery

Standard, January 9, 1845, 1.

CHAPTER 12
194 *"...the Cincinnati Morning Herald printed"*: *Cincinnati Morning Herald*, February 7, 1845, 3.
199 *"The Sandusky Clarion"*: *The Sandusky Clarion*, January 20, 1846, 1.

CHAPTER 13
201 *"It has been written"*: Mahan, Erastus. *Friends of Liberty on the Mackinaw*. McClean County (Ill.) Historical Society, Bloomington. Volume 1, 1899, 397. https://archive.org/details/transactionsofmc01mcle/page/n901/mode/2up?q=Mahan. Retrieved July 1, 2025.
201 *"Methodist local preacher"*: Dr. Isaac M. Beck letter to Wilbur H. Siebert, December 26, 1892. (Courtesy of Ohio History Connection.)
201 *"The Presbyterian Church split"*: Fortson, Donald S. III. *Old New Calvinism: The New School Presbyterian Spirit*. Reformed Theological Seminary, Charlotte, online. https://journal.rts.edu/article/old-new-calvinism-the-new-school-presbyterian-spirit/ Retrieved July 3, 2025.
201 *"Rankin chose the New School"*: Grim, Paul R. *The Rev. John Rankin, Early Abolitionist*. Ohio Archaeological and Historical Quarterly, Volume 46, 45. (Courtesy of Ohio History Connection.)
201 *"...tended to be more evangelistic"*: Morris, Edward, D. A Book of Remembrance: *The Presbyterian Church New School 1837-1869 an Historical Review*. Champlin Press, Columbus, Ohio. 1905, 52-60.
201 *"Rankin was listed as"*: *The History of Brown County, Ohio*. Chicago, W.H. Beers & Co., 1883, 673.
201 *"Daniel Gilmer (New School)"*: *"The Old School Chillicothe Presbytery"*: Galbraith, Rev. R.C. *The History of the Chillicothe Presbytery: From Its Organization in 1799 to 1889*. Chillicothe (Ohio), 1889, 150.
202 *"The Old School Chillicothe Presbytery"*: Galbraith, Rev. R.C. *The History of the Chillicothe Presbytery: From Its Organization in 1799 to 1889*. Chillicothe (Ohio), 1889.
202 *"...the surname of Hamilton"*: *The History of Brown County, Ohio*. Chicago, W.H. Beers & Co., 1883, 674.
202 *"Beck was Disciples of Christ"*: Dr. Isaac M. Beck letter to Wilbur H. Siebert, December 26, 1892. (Courtesy of Ohio History Connection.)
202 *"...to worship with the Baptists"*: *The History of Brown County, Ohio*. Chicago, W.H. Beers & Co., 1883, 674.

203 *"Rev. Daniel Gilmer"*: Galbraith, Rev. R.C. *The History of the Chillicothe Presbytery: From Its Organization in 1799 to 1889.* Chillicothe (Ohio), 1889, 151.

203 *"James Gilliland did the same"*: Ibid., 144.

203 *"Samuel G. Moore was affiliated"*: Note: *The History of the Chillicothe Presbytery* never mentioned the Russellville church left the Old School for New School, but the Chillicothe Presbytery never refers once to Rev. Lockhart or the Russellville church after 1839.

203 *"Christian Donaldson owned a Cincinnati"*: *Cincinnati Daily Gazette*, January 20 1842, 3,

203 *"Ohio Anti-Slavery Society executive committee"*: *The Philanthropist*, June 12 1838, 5.

203 *"Only John R. Strain"*: Galbraith, Rev. R.C. *The History of the Chillicothe Presbytery: From Its Organization in 1799 to 1889.* Chillicothe (Ohio), 1889, 353.

203 *"Christian Donaldson became a member"*: *Tri Weekly Cincinnati Gazette*, January 4, 1845, 2.

BIBLIOGRAPHY

Birney, William. *James G. Birney and His Times: the genesis of the republican party with some account of abolition movements in the south before 1828.* New York: D. Appleton and Company, 1890.

Cochran, William, C. *The Western Reserve and the Fugitive Slave Law.* Cleveland. The Western Reserve Historical Society, Publication No. 101, 1920.

Coleman, J. Winston Jr. *Slavery Times in Kentucky.* Chapel Hill, N.C. The University of North Carolina press, 1940.

Debate at the Lane Seminary, Cincinnati, Speech of James A. Thome, of Kentucky, at the Annual Meeting of the American Anti-Slavery Society, May 6, 1834. Letter of the Rev. Dr. Samuel H. Cox, Against the American Colonization Society. Boston, Garrison & Knapp, 1834.

Foner, Eric. *Free soil, free labor, free men: the ideology of the Republican Party before the Civil War.* New York, Oxford Press, 1979.

Galbraith, Rev. R.C. *The History of the Chillicothe Presbytery: From Its Organization in 1799 to 1889.* Chillicothe (Ohio), 1889.

Grant, U.S. *Personal Memoirs of U.S. Grant.* Old Saybrook (Conn.), Konecky & Konecky, 1885.

Hagedorn, Ann. *Beyond the River: The Untold Story of the Heroes of the Underground Railroad.* New York, Simon & Schuster, 2002.

Hodges, Albert G. *A Digest of the Statute Laws of Kentucky.* Frankfort, 1842.

Johnson, Paul. *A History of the American People.* New York, Harper Collins, 1997.

Johnson, Reinhard O. *The Liberty Party, 1840–1848: Antislavery Third-Party Politics in the United States.* United States: LSU Press, 2009.

Journal of the Senate of Ohio, as the First Session of the Thirty-Seventh General Assembly; Held in the City of Columbus, and Commencing Monday, December 3, 1838. Columbus, 1838-39, 393.

Mahan, Erastus. *Friends of Liberty on the Mackinaw.* McClean County (Ill.) Historical Society, Bloomington. Volume 1, 1899. https://archive.org/details/transactionsofmc01mcle/page/n901/mode/2up?q=Mahan. Retrieved July 1, 2025.

McCullough, David. *The Pioneers: The Heroic Story of the Settlers Who*

Brought the American Ideal West. New York, Simon & Schuster, 2019.

McCutcheon, Marc. *The Writer's Guide to Everyday Life in the 1800s.* Cincinnati, Writer's Digest Books, 1993.

Morris, B.F. *The Life of Thomas Morris: Pioneer and long a legislator of Ohio and U.S. Senator from 1833 to 1839.* Cincinnati: Moore, Wilstach, Keys & Overend, 1856.

Morris, Edward, D. *A Book of Remembrance: The Presbyterian Church New School 1837-1869 an Historical Review.* Champlin Press, Columbus, Ohio. 1905.

Ohio Anti-Slavery Convention. *Proceedings of the Ohio Anti-Slavery Convention. Held at Putnam, on the twenty-second, twenty-third, and twenty-fourth of April, 1835.* Putnam, 1835.

Reid, Joseph B. and Reeder, Henry R. *Trial of Rev. John B. Mahan, for felony: in the Mason Circuit Court of Kentucky: commencing on Tuesday, the 13th, and terminating on Monday the 19th of November, 1838.* Cincinnati, 1838.

Russell, Thomas H. *The Illustrious Life and Work of Warren G. Harding, Twenty-Ninth President of the United States: From Farm to White House.* 1923

Stephens, Alexander H. *A Compendium of the History of the United States from the Earliest Settlements to 1872.* American Foundation Publication, Bridgewater, Va. 1999.

The History of Brown County, Ohio. Chicago, W.H. Beers & Co., 1883.

Thompson, Carl N. *Historical Collections of Brown County*, Hammer Graphics, Piqua (Ohio), 1969.

Van Deusen, Glyndon G. *The Life of Henry Clay.* Little, Brown and Company, Boston, 1937.

Wardlaw, Joseph G. *Genealogy of the Wardlaw Family: with some account of other families with which it is connected.* York, South Carolina, 1929.

Wilmore, Rev. August Cleland. *History of the White River Conference of the United Brethren in Christ.* Church of the United Brethren in Christ United Brethren Publishing House, Dayton, 1925.

ARTICLES

Fortson, Donald S. III. *Old New Calvinism: The New School Presbyterian Spirit.* Reformed Theological Seminary, Charlotte. https://journal.rts.edu/article/old-new-calvinism-the-new-school-presbyterian-spirit/ Retrieved July 3, 2025.

Grim, Paul R. *The Rev. John Rankin, Early Abolitionist.* Ohio Archaeological and Historical Quarterly, Volume 46. (Courtesy of Ohio

History Connection.)

Hand, Greg. *Cincinnati Magazine.* February 18, 2016.

McGroarty, William Buckner. *Exploration in Mass Emancipation.* The William and Mary College Quarterly Historical Magazine, Volume 21(3).

Powell, C. A., Kavanaugh, B. T., and Christy, D. *Transplanting Free Negroes to Ohio from 1815 to 1858.* The Journal of Negro History, 1916, 1(3).

Preston, Emmett D. *The Fugitive Slave Acts in Ohio.* The Journal of Negro History, Volume 28(4).

Rivington, Kate. *In its Midst: An Analysis of One Hundred Southern-Born Anti-Slavery Activists.* Australasian Journal of American Studies, Volume 38 (1).

Salafia, Matthew. *Searching for Slavery: Fugitive Slaves in the Ohio River Valley Borderland, 1830–1860.* Ohio Valley History, Volume 8(4).

Siebert, Wilbur H. *Beginnings of the Underground Railroad in Ohio.* Ohio Archaeological and Historical Quarterly, Volume 56 (1). (Courtesy of Ohio History Connection.)

Volpe, Vernon L. *The Ohio Election of 1838: Study in the Historical Method?* https://resources.ohiohistory.org/ohj/search/display.php?page=46&searchterm =105th&vol=95&p ages=85-100 Retrieved July 2, 2025. (Courtesy of Ohio History Connection.)

Wyatt-Brown, Bertram. *The Abolitionists' Postal Campaign of 1835.* The Journal of Negro History Volume 50(4).

LETTERS

Dr. Isaac M. Beck letter to Wilbur H. Siebert, December 26, 1892. (Courtesy of Ohio History Connection.)

Morgan Neville letter to Thomas Jefferson, December 10, 1819. National Archives, Founders Online. https://founders.archives.gov/documents/Jefferson/03-15-02-0246 Retrieved July 1, 2025.

NEWSPAPERS

Baltimore Sun
Carroll Free Press
Cincinnati Enquirer
Cincinnati Morning Herald
Clermont Courier

Cleveland Daily Herald
Cleveland Daily Herald and Gazette
Cleveland Weekly Plain Dealer
Flemingsburg Kentuckian
Georgetown Democratic Standard
Greene County Gazette
The Liberty Hall and Cincinnati Gazette
Maumee City Express
Oberlin Evangelist
The Liberator
The National Anti-Slavery Standard
The Philanthropist
The Rochester Freeman
The Sandusky Clarion
Troy Times
Urbana Democrat and Herald
Vermont State Journal
Vermont Telegraph
Western Citizen
Wilmington Democrat and Herald

DISSERTATION/THESIS

Hur, Hyun. *Radical Antislavery and Personal Liberty Laws in Antebellum Ohio, 1803-1857*. PhD dissertation, Univ. of Wisconsin, 2012.

Parker, Edmond Thomas, *The Methodist Circuit Rider in the Old Northwest*, 1966, Master's thesis. https://ecommons.luc.edu/luc_theses/2186 Retrieved July 1, 2025.

NAME INDEX

Adams, John Quincy—45, 143.
Atherton, Charles—136.
Bailey, Dr. Gamaliel—98, 182.
Beck, Dr. Isaac—9, 11, 36-37, 39, 44, 54-57, 59-60, 72, 105, 126, 137, 153, 156, 169, 177, 182, 186-187, 191, 201-202.
Beham, Joseph—31.
Bender, Adam—187.
Birney, James G.—9, 24, 26-27, 29-32, 35, 45, 47, 50, 55, 68, 177, 183.
"Black Bill" —184-185.
Bollman, Erick—96.
Bowen, Judge Ozias—184.
Bradley, James—45-47.
Brodrick, James—106.
Bronnough, David—117-118.
Burnet, Judge—31.
Burr, Aaron—26, 96.
Campbell, Alexander—72, 126, 183.
Carberry, Valentine—155, 159, 160.
Carr, Samuel—106.
Chambers, Francis—102.
Chambers, John—90, 102-103, 109-118, 122.
Clark, Gov. James—72-73, 82-84, 95, 102, 169, 174.
Clark, Samuel—106.
Clay, Sen. Henry—65, 137.
Cliff, Hensley—106.
Coffin, Levi—9.

Colby (surname) —30.
Collins, Rev. John—131.
Collins, Richard—131.
Corothers (surname) —57.
Crabb, Vince—74.
Cumberland, Jacob—155, 156, 160, 191.
Cumberland, James—169.
Cumberland, Moses—155.
Cutler, Ephraim—20.
Davies, Mayor Samuel—31-32,
Devore, Ann—166, 171-172, 174.
Dobbins, Rev.—57.
Donaldson, Christian—29, 196.
Douglass, Absalom—183.
Downing, Reason—106.
Dunham, John—46.
Dunlap, William—133, 177, 188-190, 195.
Evans, E.P. —196, 199.
Fox, Arthur—44.
Fox, Tom—154, 156.
Frazier, William—59, 126.
Galbraith, Nathan—47.
Garrison, William Lloyd—10, 58.
Gilliland, Rev. James—57, 58, 90, 196.
Gilliland, S.W. —59.
Gilmer, Rev. Daniel—196, 199, 201.
Gist, Mary—41.

Gist, Samuel—40-41.
Graham, David—54.
Graham, Joseph—31.
Grant, Ulysses—8, 88-89.
Greathouse, William—74-75, 102-104, 107-112, 114-117, 120, 122, 124, 126, 128, 131-133, 135, 138, 158-159, 162-164, 166-173, 179, 188-190, 197.
Hamer, Thomas—55, 70, 74, 87- 89, 126, 156-157, 159, 162, 190.
Hamilton (surname)—104-106, 202.
Harding, Warren G. —70.
Henderson, David—106.
Hibbens, Thomas—104.
Hill, John—117-118.
Howe, Joseph—106.
Howe, Spencer R. —106.
Huber, C.B. —183.
Hudson, John—11, 43, 59, 63, 95, 105, 109, 155.
Hudson, Sally—155-157.
Huggins, A. —173.
Huggins, James—43, 169, 173.
Huggins, Robert—63, 155.
Keys, Colonel—61.
Johnson, Pres. Andrew—143.
Johnson, Eliza Jane—43-44, 91, 94, 98-99, 101-102, 105, 116.
Jolliffe, John—182.
Kincaid, Esquire—64.
Kratzer, James—157.
La Rue, Thomas—106.
Lewis, John—184.

Lincoln, Abraham—11, 89.
Lindsey, Grant—155.
Lockhart, Rev.—57.
Lovejoy, Elijah—90, 176.
Mahan, Alexander—192-193.
Mahan, Ann Eliza—192-193.
Mahan, Asa—45.
Mahan, Erastus—38.
Mahan, Isaac—192-193.
Mahan, Rev. Jacob—34.
Mahan, Rev. John B. —8-15 (Introduction), 16-17 (Photos), 18-19, 22, 24-25, 33-40, 42-45, 47, 50-55, 57, 67, 70, 72-75, 76-82 (Letters from prison), 83-86, 88-91, 95-101, 103-104, 106-113, 116, 118-119, 121-124, 126--132 (Post-trial letter), 133-134, 137-140, 143-144, 153-165 (Second trial), 166-174 (Third trial), 177, 178-180 (Shaw letter), 182-183, 186-193, (Last days and will and testament), 194-198, 200-203.
Mahan, John Wesley—192-193.
Mahan, Martha—36, 192-193
Mahan, Mary Jane—188, 190, 192.
Mahan, Polly—35, 37-38, 76-80, 105, (Letters from prison), 191, 193.
Mahan, Russel Bigelow—192-193.
Mahan, William—35-36, 105.
Masters, Samuel—103, 105.
McClanahan, John—61.
McClean, John—188, 190.
McCoy, William—126, 182.

McClung, John—102.
Meek, Rev. John—170.
Miller, Lewis—196.
Moore, Josiah—9, 11, 37, 54, 59, 169, 182-183, 191, 194, 196, 199.
Moore, Samuel—196.
Morehead, James T. —140-141.
Morgan, John—89.
Morris, Benjamin—183.
Morris, Ohio Rep. Isaiah—141-142,
Morris, U.S. Sen. Thomas—44, 55, 86, 100, 137, 142, 153, 159, 176, 183, 185-186.
Myers, J.W.J. —173.
Nelson, John—61.
Neville, Morgan—26.
Nevin, Andrew—38.
Pangburn, Rev. Hampton—202.
Parry, Thomas—106.
Payne, Thomas—102, 104-105, 108-109, 112-114, 116-118, 122.
Perrigo, James—107-110, 112, 114-117, 120-123, 128, 130-131, 166-167, 169-172, 174.
Pettijohn, Abraham—42, 47, 50-51, 59, 63.
Pettijohn, Amos—54, 126, 155, 164.
Pettijohn, Joseph—155, 160, 164.
Pettijohn, Lewis—75, 169, 173.
Pettijohn Family—11, 105, 159, 191.
Polk, President James—188.

Prater, George W. —106.
Price, Judge John W. —157.
Purdum, Mr. —161-162.
Rankin, Rev. John —10-11, 24, 38, 45, 47, 50-52, 57-58, 72, 90, 126, 191, 201.
Rankin, Rev. Samuel—202.
Reid, Judge Walker—91-97, 103, 105-107, 119-120, 123, 125, 129.
Riggs, Stephen—47.
Rush, Dr. Benjamin—187.
Rutherford, Rev. Robert—47.
Sewal, David—61.
Shannon, Gov. Wilson—140.
Shaw, James—178.
Smith, J. Speed—140-141
Steele, Rev. —57.
Stowe, Harriet Beecher—10-11, 45.
Strain, John—196.
Swartwout, Samuel—96.
Tappan, Arthur—52.
Tappan, Benjamin—52, 137, 153.
Taylor, John—102.
Taylor, William—62.
Turner, Nat—58.
Vance, Gov. Joseph—12-14, 43, 72-73, 82-84, 86-88, 95, 102, 105, 133, 134-136, (Statement about Mahan), 169, 174, 176.
Vaughan, John—90, 102, 113, 119-120.
Wade, Ohio Sen. Benjamin—140-143.
Waller, Henry—102, 120-121.

Wardlaw, Robert—33.
Washington, George—20.
Watson, Samuel—106.
Weld, Theodore—45, 40,
White, Ohio Sen. Charles—142.
Wood, Sheriff David—73, 82, 85.
Young, David—33.

ABOUT THE AUTHOR

Daniel J. Vance grew up visiting Sardinia relatives every two weeks. He has fond memories of the village, including ordering peanut butter milkshakes at Pat's Dairy Bar, watching his cousin Steve fill the town water tower, and getting his hair cut at Ken's Barber Shop. He is a semi-retired Licensed Professional Clinical Counselor, was editor of *Connect Business Magazine* nineteen years, author of the nationally self-syndicated newspaper column *Disabilities* fifteen years, and has authored or ghost-written a number of books, including *Unique Mankato Stories*. He lives in rural Minnesota with wife Carolyn. He also one day may write about his paternal great-grandmother's uncle, Rev. Jonathan Knowlton Wellman, a New York City magazine publisher and 1850s Michigan abolitionist; and about the nationally (and wrongly) discredited Ohio 60th Volunteer Infantry and their experience at the Civil War Battle of Harper's Ferry. He can be reached via danieljvance@gmail.com.

ACKNOWLEDGEMENTS

The author wishes to thank members of the Sardinia Historical Society, including Patsy Albert, Randi York, and Sandra Purdy, for their help in bringing this project to fruition; Rev. John B. Mahan, for his accomplishments despite unbearable personal suffering; the late Stanley Mignerey Jr., the author's uncle and former Sardinia mayor, for sharing his knowledge about a Sardinia "slave tunnel" and his business interactions with Gist Settlement descendants in the 1950s; Ohio History Connection; Kristina Estle, Thomas Homans, Dr. William Trollinger, and Sandra Purdy for their endorsements; and the person years ago responsible for erecting the Sardinia historical highway marker honoring John Bennington Mahan—without which this book never would have been written.

www.ingramcontent.com/pod-product-compliance
Lightning Source LLC
Chambersburg PA
CBHW070644160426
43194CB00009B/1570